The Trench

Life and Death on the Western Front
1914-1918

Trevor Yorke

Foreword by Michael Morpurgo

COUNTRYSIDE BOOKS
NEWBURY, BERKSHIRE

First published 2014
© Trevor Yorke 2014
Reprinted 2014 (Twice)

COUNTRYSIDE BOOKS
3 Catherine Road
Newbury, Berkshire

To view our complete range of books,
please visit us at www.countrysidebooks.co.uk

ISBN 978 1 84674 3177

The front cover photograph shows
4th E. Lancs Rgt troops in 1917 (I.W.M.).

Photograph of Gallipoli trench on page 50 by Steve Jacques.

Photograph of poppies on page 96 by Dr Carol Cooper.

With many thanks to Michael Bode for his assistance in compiling this book.

Maps and illustrations by the author.

Designed by Roger Davis, Kingsclere Design and Print
Produced by The Letterworks Ltd, Reading
Printed by Berforts Information Press, Oxford

Contents

Foreword by Michael Morpurgo   5

Introduction   7

Chapter 1
Opening Moves
Battle Lines are Drawn   11

Chapter 2
The Trenches
Design and Construction   17

Chapter 3
Life in the Trench
Eating, Sleeping and Staying Alive   31

Chapter 4
Trench Warfare
Tactics, Weapons and Tanks   47

Chapter 5
Going Home
1918 and the Aftermath of War   73

Appendix 1: The Origins of the First World War   84

Appendix 2: Places to Visit   89

Glossary of Terms   92

Index   94

The Menin Gate Memorial to the Missing at Ypres

This dignified building of remembrance is dedicated to those British and Commonwealth soldiers who were killed in action locally and who have no known grave. It was built by the Commonwealth War Graves Commission and unveiled in 1927. Ypres was of strategic importance during the First World War and no fewer than five major battles were fought around it. By the end of the fighting the town was a ruined shell and the allies had lost some 300,000 men in the Ypres Salient. The bodies of 90,000 of these were never recovered. German losses around Ypres during the war are thought to be around 200,000. Every evening at 8 pm the road through the gate is closed and buglers from the town's fire brigade sound the 'Last Post'.

Foreword by

Michael Morpurgo

The picture opposite is of the Menin Gate at Ypres in Belgium. The caption speaks for itself. Ypres is a sad town but an enormously positive one. It's one of the places that has grown out of its wartime ruins. I find it very moving that its inhabitants have taken the time and the trouble, and have had the spirit to rebuild their town, which was largely destroyed in the Great War. In my mind, it symbolises hope.

Ypres isn't the sort of place you go simply to enjoy yourself. You go for the experience – and I think all young people should visit the town and its surrounding cemeteries. You must also visit the excellent *In Flanders Fields* museum there, which is one of the best museums about the Great War that I've ever visited. It doesn't seek to glorify the war in any way, it just tells it as it was - and I'd urge any visitor to the town to go there and perhaps take along the children (if they're old enough), in order to give them a better understanding of this most terrible of conflicts.

I always also visit at least one of the wartime cemeteries outside Ypres. Indeed, I came across the name of a Private Peaceful at one such cemetery, and it was that which inspired my book of the same name.

When I came to write *War Horse*, I decided I would tell the story of that war seen through the eyes of a horse. Joey, I would call him. It would be an English story, but a German one too, and a French one. It would be a tale, as far as possible, of the universal suffering, not just in that war, but in all wars, and on all sides. That is the spirit in which the book was written, and in which the play is acted out now each night, not only in London and in the US, but also now in Berlin.

To tell the story is the only way we have left to remember, and the only way to pass it on. And it is important to pass it on, important for the men who died on all sides, all now unknown soldiers, for those who suffered long afterwards and grieved all their lives. And important for us too. If they gave their todays for our tomorrows, then, I am sure, after all they went through, and died for, they would wish to see us doing all we can to create a world of peace and goodwill, a world that one day will turn its back on war for good.

It is through their words and our stories that we must and will remember this and remember them. Then we really will be honouring their memory.

In 2014, as we begin to mark the centenary of the First World War, we should honour those who died, most certainly, and gratefully too, but we should never glorify. We should heed the words of those who were there, who did the fighting, and some of them the dying. To Wilfred Owen, the words Horace had used to glorify war centuries before, 'Dulce et decorum est pro patria mori' - how sweet and fitting it is to die for your country - were simply 'the old lie'.

During these next four years of commemoration we should read the poems, the stories, the history, the diaries, visit the cemeteries - German cemeteries as well as ours - they were all sons and brothers and lovers and husbands and fathers too.

There should be no flag waving, unless it be the lowering of the flags of all the nations who lost their sons, unless it be to celebrate the peace we now share together, unless it be to reaffirm again our determination to guard our freedom, but as far as humanly possible to do it in peace. And when we sing the anthems, let them be anthems of peace and reconciliation.

Come each November over the next four years, let the red poppy and the white poppy be worn together to honour those who died, to keep our faith with them, to make of this world a place where freedom and peace can reign together.

Michael Morpurgo

Introduction

Sepia photos of uniformed relatives in family albums; silent images from old newsreels of soldiers trudging through muddy trenches, and pictures of field artillery on wooden gun carriages, can make the First World War seem distant and irrelevant in the modern world. Current media has given a verdict that the war was run by pompous generals with outrageous moustaches and a nonchalant disrespect for life as they sent thousands of trusting soldiers to a casual oblivion. The scale of the conflict and the suffering it produced is frightening not only because of those lost on the front lines but through the millions of men, women and animals who also suffered in what seems a largely pointless war.

At the time however, the First World War appeared new and challenging. Rapid developments in weaponry, armoured vehicles, aircraft, chemical warfare and defensive measures pushed designers and industrialists to the limits. Military planners and officers in the field were constantly revising tactics and devising new ways of coordinating their forces. Politicians and commanders had to try and predict the enemy's next move while juggling their colossal fighting machines over the numerous fronts of the wide empires they controlled. The decisions made by these same leaders in the period immediately after the war ended has not only created conflict and tensions which are still felt today, but also began an irrevocable change in the world from one of monarchy and empire to democracy and independence.

Despite the global aspect of the First World War (and the war was indeed global in that few countries in the world were not impacted in some way by it) this book concentrates upon what became known as the Western Front, where Germans became locked in combat with French, Belgian, British, and British Empire forces along a huge 450 mile complex of trenches. These were the killing fields between 1914 and 1918.

Whether you are a student tackling the subject for the first time or wish to know more about the conditions endured by a long departed relative caught up in the conflict, I have set out to explain the war in the trenches using easy to understand text and clearly labelled drawings.

The Western Front: A map showing the course of the Western Front with a Union Jack centred on the section which was manned by the British Forces. The exact location of the trenches and the length of the front patrolled by a certain country varied through the war so this representation is only approximate. The Front also continued south east from Verdun down to the border with Switzerland. It is important to note that the section highlighted as British was also manned by forces from Canada, Australia, New Zealand, India, South Africa and other parts of the Empire as well as soldiers from Allied countries including France and Portugal and construction workers from China. This emphasises the global scale of the conflict even though this area of the First World War was confined to the north east of France .

: British : French : German

: Allied territory : Germany / Triple Alliance : Neutral Countries

o : Towns, cities and battlesites : Important rivers

I have placed the chapter which explains the origins of the war – always a daunting subject unless you already have a basic understanding of 19th century European history – as an Appendix at the end of the book, rather than at the beginning. Hopefully, this will allow readers to become more easily involved with the subject, especially if they have no previous military knowledge. The first chapter describes the early movement of the various combatants as the war began and why the war so quickly developed into a stalemate of trench warfare.

4th East Lancs saphead
Givenchy, January 1918.

The second chapter looks in detail at the trenches, their features and how they were built under enemy fire. The third shows what daily life was like, from simple domestic chores to the dangerous raids the soldiers had to undertake. The fourth chapter examines the tactics which developed during the war and explains how the different types of weapons worked. The final chapter outlines the closing stages of the war, its aftermath, and the way in which The Lost were remembered. Within these chapters are boxed-out stories of the key battles of the war. There is a list of museums and places to visit, including the main battle sites in France and Belgium. I have also detailed websites where you can find more information for further research.

If I have learnt anything from writing this book it is that preconceptions are dangerous. Put aside any thought that this war was a boring, predictable stalemate and prepare to be surprised, impressed and horrified by what you find. Hopefully, the book will ignite a new respect for those of every level and nationality who gave their lives for their country, 'Lest we forget'.

Trevor Yorke

Structure	Approximate Size	Officers in Order of Rank
ARMY		FIELD MARSHAL
CORPS:	(50,000 men)	GENERAL
		LIEUTENANT GENERAL
DIVISION:	(16-18,000 men)	MAJOR GENERAL
BRIGADE:	(3-4,000 men)	BRIGADIER GENERAL
		COLONEL
BATTALION:	(800-1,000 men)	LIEUTENANT COLONEL
COMPANY:	(160-200 men)	MAJOR
		CAPTAIN
PLATOON:	(40-50 men)	LIEUTENANT
SECTION:	(10-14 men)	2ND LIEUTENANT

A British Army structure chart during the First World War is shown on the left with a list of the officers in order of their rank on the right. A length of the front was assigned to an army corps (from the Latin word *corpus* meaning 'body') which would usually be made up of three divisions, two of which would man the front and one the reserve trenches. This dividing and rotating of groups between the front and reserve trenches was mirrored all the way down the structure to the platoon. A regiment was the largest permanent grouping of men within the British Army in peacetime, but in the war the battalions of which they were made up did not necessarily fight alongside each other.

Opening Moves
Battle Lines are Drawn

The British Army in August 1914 consisted of a volunteer force of some 400,000 officers and men. It was well trained and equipped, with around half its number devoted to maintaining stability around the British Empire. Just as important was the Royal Navy, defending and linking the colonies together and ensuring that trade could flourish and carry forward the benefits of the new science and technology which the Victorian era had created.

The last thing wanted was a European war. These were surely episodes of past history, and Britain now had a global theatre to be concerned with.

Europe with the Allies marked in yellow and the Central Powers in orange. The shaded countries joined the respective coloured sides after 1914, those in white remained neutral. Germany had the problem of two fronts on land to deal with. Its access to the Atlantic was blocked by Britain, which made it vulnerable to having supply ships blockaded by the Allies.

So it was ironic that the First World War began with the assassination of an Archduke in Sarajevo, Serbia, in circumstances of pantomime proportions in July 1914. For details, see Appendix 1 The Origins of the First World War, on page 84.

Unfortunately, Franz Ferdinand was the heir to the Austro–Hungarian Empire, which had links and treaties with European nations that could and did drag all of them into conflict.

Austria-Hungary used the assassination of Archduke Ferdinand as an opportunity to stamp its authority upon the Serbians. The Austro-Hungarian government accused the Serbian government of being behind the plot and on the 23rd July 1914, they delivered an ultimatum demanding access into Serbia to carry out a judicial review. The Serbians proposed arbitration and upon hearing this, the German Kaiser wrote, 'A great moral victory for Vienna; but every pretext for war falls to the ground.' But Austria-Hungary had no intention of waiting and on 28th July they declared war on Serbia. Within two days their artillery was firing at the Serbian capital of Belgrade. The Russians, bound by treaty to Serbia, had already begun to mobilise, despite a warning from Germany that they would counter any efforts they made to support Serbia. The Kaiser was now convinced that the Triple Entente nations (Britain, France and Russia) were manipulating events in order to draw Germany into war. On the 2nd August, Germany, allied to Austria-Hungary by treaty, declared war on Russia and then invaded neutral Belgium, declaring war on France at the same time. Britain initially emphasised that her Entente Cordiale with France was only an understanding, but fearful that a victorious Germany would be calamitous for British interests, they used an 1839 treaty protecting Belgian neutrality as a pretext to declare war on Germany two days later.

Kitchener's call for volunteers: unlike many at the time, he thought the war could last for years rather than months, and fronted a massive recruitment campaign to build up a suitably large army.

All sides assumed, like previous wars, that 'it would be over by Christmas' and prepared themselves for fast moving, mobile warfare.

The Schlieffen Plan

The German army had over 700,000 troops. As there was universal conscription for young men in the country, they could call up a further three million reservists within a week of the beginning of the war. They also had a plan, devised by Count Alfred von Schlieffen, their Chief of Staff up until 1906, which tried to solve their problem of an enemy on both their East and West Fronts. Von Schlieffen presumed that the Russians would be slow to mobilise and that the French would try and claim back their former lands in Lorraine and Alsace first. He advised that the German army should therefore pass through Holland and Belgium and then swing round the back of Paris, capturing the capital and trapping the French army in one vast pincer movement. They could then send their forces to the Eastern Front to deal with the later threat from Russia. However, the new Chief of Staff, Helmuth von Moltke, amended the plan by taking a more challenging route directly into Belgium. The result was that the Germans were held up for nearly two weeks trying to take stoutly defended forts and did not enter Brussels until 14th August.

This delay gave the French additional time to prepare their army. It was of a similar size to the Germans', containing experienced soldiers from North African conflicts with a special skill for dash in attack. The French 'Plan 17' concentrated their forces upon an attack into Lorraine and Alsace, as von Schlieffen had predicted, and they assumed that the Germans would not invade via Belgium. On 14th August, their forces rolled across the border but were forced back by German heavy artillery and machine guns, suffering around 300,000 casualties in just two weeks of fighting.

To the north, the British Expeditionary Army of just over 100,000 men had landed and clashed with the German forces at Mons, Belgium on 23rd August. Despite inflicting heavy casualties due to their excellent rifle skills, the British were heavily outnumbered and began to fall back and meet up with the retreating French forces. However, the German plan was already in trouble. Its huge sweeping movement designed to capture Paris was falling short and they were having problems getting sufficient supplies to the front line. In addition, the Russians surprised them with the speed of their mobilisation by launching an offensive on the Germans' Eastern Front, which then obliged them to take resources away from the west in order to force the Russians back.

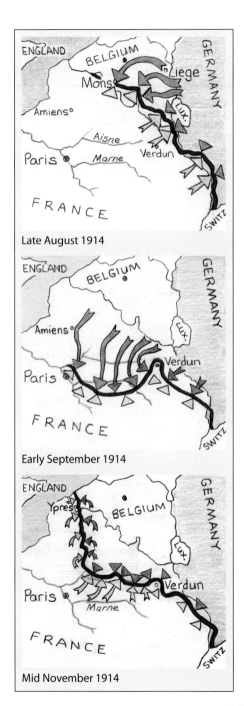

Late August 1914

Early September 1914

Mid November 1914

The Western Front Becomes Entrenched

The French quickly reassembled an army and, along with the British forces, pushed the Germans back from the east of Paris in what came to be referred to as the Miracle of the Marne. The German forces retreated to the next defendable line, the river Aisne, where they were able to select high ground and dig themselves in, creating a formidable barrier which held the allied forces at bay. Unable to breach this line they too had to build trenches to keep their men out of the firing line of enemy artillery and gun fire. This left a large gap to the north and both armies tried to go round the side of each other (outflanking) in the Race to the Sea. This was a series of offensives which continued into November 1914 when the coast was reached. As winter was closing in and both sides were exhausted, the Allied and German forces dug lines

These three maps show the movement of the armies and position of the Western Front (marked in red) during the turbulent fighting of late summer and autumn 1914.

The final map shows the Race to the Sea as both sides tried to outflank each other, together with what was to be the approximate position of the Front for the following three years.

of trenches to hold their positions and so formed a vast barrier which stretched from the Belgian coast down to the border with Switzerland in the south, a distance of around 400 miles. The more defensive-minded Germans had taken vast swathes of Belgium and northern France and here they built more permanent defences. The Allies, who saw this as just a temporary halt to proceedings, dug less substantial trench systems, confident that in the following spring offensive they would be marching on towards Berlin. Few who constructed, lived and fought minor skirmishes and raids through that first winter envisaged that the grim, muddy hell hole which they had created was to be their home for much of the next three and a half years.

> ## 'I adore war. It is like a big picnic but without the objectivelessness of a picnic. I have never been more well or more happy.'
>
> **Captain Julian Grenfell,**
> October 1914
>
> Julian Grenfell wrote enthusiastically about going to war and this quote triggered arguments in the press about the way it encouraged men to sign up under a false understanding of what they would face at the front.
>
> This talented poet died in May 1915 when a shell fragment hit his head. His brother was killed two months later only a mile from where Julian had been struck down.

Princess Mary's Gift Box
Christmas, 1914

This small brass box with a beautifully embossed lid contained tobacco or sweets and chocolate for everyone serving in uniform on Christmas Day, 1914. It also came with a greetings card from the Princess that looked forward to a Victorious New Year. The boxes were paid for by public subscription and nearly 400,000 were delivered by the due date.

Border Regiment soldiers in dug-outs,
the Somme, 1916.

Royal Artillery trench cookers,
Wancourt, 1917.

Sappers fixing scaling ladders,
Arras, 1917.

Chapter 2

The Trenches
Design and Construction

As the huge opposing armies became entrenched during late 1914, only a few of their military leaders might have had the words of a Polish banker, Jan Gotlib Bloch, ringing in their ears. He had spent many years studying modern warfare and predicted that this conflict would begin with a terrible slaughter then be followed by a stalemate; modern artillery and rapid firing weapons would make this war one of entrenchment. Bloch had even calculated that the soldier within a trench had a four-fold advantage over the infantryman advancing towards him and that millions of fighting men would become involved. The war would take years rather than months to resolve and would be won through industrial might, economic attrition and the blockading of supplies. These remarkably accurate predictions should not have surprised many had they been made in 1914 as the sides went to war, but Bloch had been dead for twelve years and the book in which he had made his assessment was written in the 1890s!

Such was the confidence of the military leaders that a decisive victory would be theirs within a short time that they did not pay much attention to such warnings or prepare themselves should the sides become entrenched. They also failed to take into consideration the impact of new weaponry like the machine gun and heavy artillery.

Jan Gotlib Bloch used social, economic and scientific calculations rather than a knowledge of military tactics to put together his predictions on future war which he promoted and distributed during the final years of his life. The military largely ignored them, not only because he was not from their class but also because they did not want these ideas demoralising their forces. His belief that war was now futile because of the destructive power of modern weapons and that peaceful means of settling disputes would have to be sought were way ahead of his time.

Bloch's predictions were not just theory; the idea of digging trenches in a battlefield to hold a position was nothing new. They had been constructed for centuries as part of siege warfare, and during the American Civil War and the Russian-Japanese battle over Korea their value in protecting soldiers from modern weaponry and for holding off an attack were well appreciated. The Germans studied the events of this latter conflict and had made something of a science of the design and construction of defensive structures. The British soldiers on the other hand, were trained to dig scrapes, shallow pits in which they could lie down to shoot from, and had dug simple defensive trenches in the Boer War in South Africa at the turn of the 20th century. New recruits were trained to dig trenches before they left for the Western Front, but now they would have to carry out this work on a scale never seen before, under fire from the enemy, digging at night to avoid being shot and creating a complex system of trenches with often only the materials they could find in their locality.

Digging Trenches

As the Western Front became fixed during autumn 1914, it was usually the Germans who were able to select the highest or best ground, with the Allies having to dig in where they could. Ideally, the choice of location should be one where you have a clear range for firing yet are hidden from approaching soldiers. On the opposite side of a slope might be best so that the enemy only saw you as they came over the ridge, which also meant it was harder for enemy artillery to aim at you (a lesson learnt from the Boer War). In reality, there may have been insufficient time due to enemy fire to be so selective; the lie of the land and physical obstructions may have also forced the issue of where to dig. The course taken would also have to make sudden changes in direction or include certain defensive features as it met a canal, river or railway line, or worked its way through built up areas. As a result, the front line could be as close as 30 or 40 metres from the enemy or up to 270 metres away (300 yards). Later in the war, as the Germans fell back to a better constructed trench system known as the Hindenburg Line, No Man's Land between the two sides stretched out as far as a kilometre (half a mile) in some places. The other problem the rapid construction caused was poor drainage, made worse in areas like Flanders where artillery fire broke up the existing ditches. Fields that had seemed dry, quickly turned into a muddy quagmire after heavy rain,

Water and mud were a constant problem in the trenches.

flooding the trenches so that soldiers had to wade through sections in places waist deep in water. This was more than just an inconvenience as it caused serious medical problems such as Trench Foot (see Chapter 3). In later defences, more care was taken to keep the trenches dry.

Most trenches within close proximity of the enemy were excavated at night to reduce the risk of soldiers getting hit by gun fire. Some were begun by linking together scrapes, dug-outs or shell craters, others were built from scratch. Entrenching was quickest when carried out by soldiers standing in a line on the surface and digging down to create a ditch. In areas where this was too risky, a safer but slower method called sapping was used, in which a pair of soldiers extended a hole or trench outwards by digging away at one end and so not exposing their heads to gun fire. This method was also used to build temporary trenches which allowed men to retreat back to another line when under intense attack. Tunnelling was another option. It was similar to sapping, but an overhead section was left in place which could be knocked out at a later date. The soil removed from the trench could be used to build up the parapet to the front and the parados to the rear of the trench to protect the soldiers from artillery blasts. The sticky, clay-like soil was put into sacks or sandbags which were laid like bricks in overlapping courses to make the core of these short walls which could absorb bullets and shrapnel.

Most of the trenches along the Western Front were dug by hand, as in this example. The Army expected 250 metres of front line trench to be dug by around 450 men in a 6 hour night-time session. In addition to infantry soldiers and Royal Engineers, around 100,000 Chinese labourers were brought over to help with their construction. It is estimated that over 25,000 miles were created by all sides, which is enough to stretch right around the globe.

A pair of entrenching tools used in the First World War. British soldiers were expected to be able to dig themselves a shallow 30 cm deep firing position (a scrape) in an hour, using a simple tool carried round with them as in the example above on the right.

The rest of the clay was used to cover them up so they didn't stand out in the landscape. Picks, shovels and spades were carried around in the baggage train but often soldiers would have had to use their own smaller entrenching tool which was part of their kit. In some extreme cases they had to resort to whatever came to hand like mess tins and spoons.

Types of Trench

Battlefield trenches could vary in form, depth and durability, despite what army manuals and training back home had suggested they should look like. Most of the earliest were built in extreme conditions under enemy fire with limited materials and tended to be less robust. They were initially dug in straight lines with men packed in shoulder to shoulder so that when a shell landed amongst them it was carnage. Lessons were quickly learnt and a more standard design and size of trench was used, with the earlier ones rebuilt and extended.

Trenches had to be deep enough so that a soldier could stand up and walk without the risk of being hit by enemy gun fire, and wide enough so that two soldiers could pass each other. They were preferably around 3 metres deep (10 ft), although some were shallower, and nearly 2 metres wide at the top (6 ft). In areas with a high water table like Flanders, any trench more than a metre deep would soon fill with water so a shallow ditch was dug down to this level and walls of clay-filled sandbags covered with earth were built up (breastwork) on either side of the trench until the required height was achieved. To reduce the casualties when a shell landed in a trench or the enemy fired down its length (enfilade fire), wide fingers of earth called traverses were built across the trench at regular intervals of around 10 metres. This broke the line into short sections called bays, so if there was an explosion or gunfire the damage would be confined to a small area.

Sandbags

Parapet

No Man's Land and enemy trenches.

Elbow rest

Timber board revetment

Ammunition shelf / box

Exposed earth

Fire-step

Wicker or brushwood revetment.

Duck-boards

Dug-out shelter.

Water

A British trench cut away with labels highlighting its key features. The crude dug-out shelter in the side of the trench, often referred to as a funk hole, was where soldiers could grab a quick rest. Note the duck boards which were crucial to prevent the water table covering the floor of the trench. These, in the form of a raised wooden slatted floor, were a solid base for the trench. A ledge called a fire-step, was inserted just over half a metre (2 ft) above the bottom. For clarity, the drawing is shown clear of all the personal effects; weaponry, rubbish and mud which would have been present in most trenches. Those which were in an active section of the Western Front would have had the debris of war all around, used ammunition boxes, temporary supporting beams, sheets of tarpaulin and mud splattered men with weathered faces catching up on sleep wherever they could.

When viewed from the air, most First World War front line trenches appear like the crenellated top of a castle wall. An alternative was to build them in a shallow zigzag line across the landscape, which was not so effective at resisting a blast but would allow the easier movement of large items, supplies and troops. Riflemen fired through loop holes, gaps or apertures left between the sandbags which formed the parapet, while standing on a ledge called a fire step which was raised half a metre (2 ft) above the bottom of the trench. In some later examples, the parados at the back was removed so that if the trench was lost then soldiers in the next line behind could fire upon the enemy who had taken possession of it.

At the bottom, a raised wooden slatted floor (with duckboards) was usually fitted to reduce the amount of mud and water soldiers had to walk through. The sides of the trench could be left bare but this made them vulnerable to collapse so most would have been kept in place as close to vertical as possible by revetments, which were usually timber boards, corrugated iron or scrap materials found locally like doors, which were pinned back by vertical posts.

Where the water table was too high in the ground, as occurred in Flanders, a shallow trench would have been dug and the sides built up with sandbags, timber and earth, as in the example shown here. These are often referred to as command or box trenches.

A British trench map showing Allied fortifications in blue and German in red. The maps were created with the aid of the newly developed aerial photography. Due to the nature of the landscape, most of the major offensives along the Western Front which involved the British Army were concentrated around Ypres and the Somme. To help find their way around, soldiers sometimes named trenches with the title of a regiment or after a particular soldier; other times recognising a local feature in the landscape, or with names which reminded them of back home.

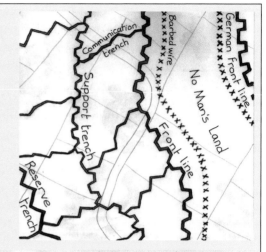

Barbed wire entanglements fixed to posts were laid out by both sides along the front of their lines (screw pickets were used later as they didn't need to be hammered in and were hence quieter to install at night). They were designed to slow an advance and make easy targets of the soldiers trying to cut their way through. Gaps were usually left so that the side which laid them out could work their way back through after making a raid. They could be completely removed at night prior to a major offensive. The wire was invented to contain cattle on the American Prairies, but the type used in the war had the barbs set much closer together than on agricultural versions so that a soldier could not get his hand between them when trying to cut it, around 16 barbs per 30 cm on German wire (their wire was also too thick for British cutters).

Sandbags were sometimes used but the trench would have to be dug wider in order to accommodate their extra width.

Although trenches may have formed a single barrier when first built, they were quickly expanded to create a complex of parallel defensive lines. This allowed soldiers to fall back to another trench if the first was lost and to use them as an area where stores and troops could stay out of harm's way during enemy artillery fire. The British usually had three lines of trenches; the front or firing line closest to the enemy, the support or travel trench around 90 metres (100 yards) or so behind this, and the reserve trench a further 200 metres (218 yards) at the rear. This was where the reserve troops could be stationed so they could counter attack if the front line was taken. These were linked by communication trenches, smaller ditches which zigzagged between the main trenches, through which soldiers and supplies could be moved back and forth.

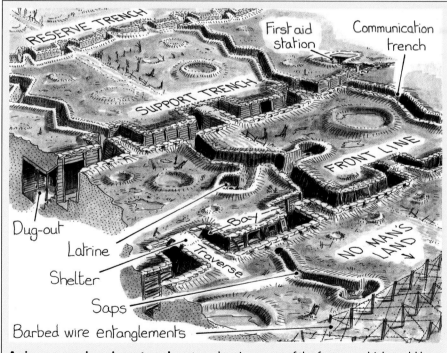

A view over an imaginary trench system showing some of the features which could be found and how they may have been arranged.

Transport during the war presented British officials with a huge logistical problem never encountered on this scale before. They had to find a way to move weapons, ammunition, food, building materials and men from French ports to the front line. Existing main line railways, rivers and canals could do part of the job but could not get close enough to the front line. The Army Service Corps with over 300,000 personnel and nearly 50,000 lorries, cars and motorbikes by the end of the war, could not shift the estimated 600 to 700 tons of stores required by each mile of trench every day. The answer

was light railways with smaller trains running at slower speeds, which as a result could be constructed quickly and be laid out at short notice to connect the front line to the main transport network. At the height of the war, the railways were moving over 150,000 tons of war materials each week and thousands of miles had been laid down with over 70,000 troops from Britain, Australia, South Africa and Canada forming companies within the Royal Engineers to run and maintain these lines.

A dug-out or bunker used for officers' accommodation and as a section command post. They were positioned at equal distances along the support trench and usually had a telephone connecting them to HQ. And of course, telephones could only function with simple land lines at the time. Some bunkers were dug as deep down as 4.5 metres (15 ft) to make them reasonably bomb proof and were lined with timber boards with stout posts supporting the beams which formed the ceiling. From here the officers could eat, sleep, organise daily routines, plan attacks, receive orders and issue commands.

26

The point where the communication trench met the front line was a potential weak point and usually had extra defensive measures to secure it. Later in the war the support trench fell from use, although it was sometimes used as a decoy to draw enemy fire. Extra trenches were also dug when an attack was imminent to house the soldiers waiting to follow after the first wave of an attack. There may have also been a further set of trenches a mile or so behind onto which troops could fall back should they be forced to retreat.

The gap between the Allied and German lines was called No Man's Land, a description which was not always accurate. Shallow trenches called saps were built out from the front line into this area so that soldiers could listen in to what the enemy was talking about, as a position for a machine gun, or as a point to launch a raid or surprise attack. The most notorious features of No Man's Land were the lines of barbed wire strung across to slow down and trap attackers so they could be more easily picked off by gun fire. These were usually set out in a pattern which was known to the defenders in order that they could find their own way through them, but formed an impenetrable wall to the charging enemy.

A replica dug-out from the Staffordshire Regiment Museum, Lichfield, Staffs. The interior is lined with timber planks and its roof held up by posts. Inside this small example are a bed, table and chair for an officer. Most built along the support trench would have been larger.

This is part of an excellent reconstructed trench system at the museum, named after L/Cpl William Coltman V.C. who had won his V.C. aged 26 in October 1918 for saving the lives of numerous comrades as they lay wounded under continuous fire. And he was an unarmed stretcher bearer! He received other medals and commendations for many similar acts of bravery and became the most decorated NCO (Non-Commissioned Officer) of the First World War.

The museum is open all year, and more details are on their website. See page 91.

Shelters and Bunkers

Within this defensive network a variety of shelters were established. Some were simply a covered section of trench which protected those beneath from heavy artillery fire (but not a direct hit) and were usually formed from pieces of timber or arched metal sheets covered in earth. The men manning the front line would try and grab sleep when conditions allowed and tended to make their own crude dug outs cut into the sides of the trench, although this could undermine the structure and their trailing legs could cause others to trip over them. The officers would expect something a little finer. Their underground shelters were usually dug down from the rear of the support trench and provided sleeping quarters, somewhere to eat and a telegraph or field telephone.

As the war progressed new, more permanent bunkers were provided so that essential work like first aid, communications and planning could take place without fear of shelling. Toilets posed a problem as soldiers were often happy just to relieve themselves where they were, causing issues with smells and disease. Latrines were provided but were usually as simple as a short passage leading to a pit, their maintenance and filling in when full were sanitary duties, often dished out to soldiers as a punishment. The concentrated odour of human waste and the quick lime spread around it made latrines unpopular, especially as some were positioned to the front of the trench and within enemy fire! Hence other solutions like old tins, buckets and even shell holes were often preferred by soldiers.

'With pick and shovel we dug trenches through beautiful fields of grain, fully realising what damage we were doing to the farmers' hopes of reaping small harvests that would enable them to stem hunger during the coming winter. The patriarch with his ox-drawn plough, the matronly gleaner, and the young woman gathering grass and leaves, roots and truffles, stood arms akimbo, wordlessly, helplessly, hopelessly watching. The depressing effect on the morale of the men – to many of whom raising grain on the Western prairie also meant their livelihood – could not be easily dismissed.'

Private Victor Wheeler
A Canadian soldier
October 1914.

28

The Second Battle of Ypres: 22nd April to 25th May 1915

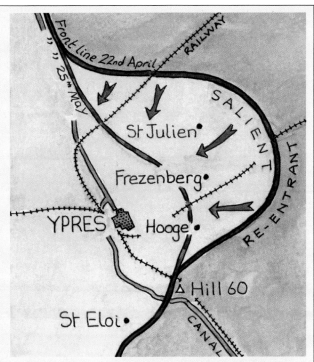

At a number of points along the Western Front the line pushed into enemy territory to wrap around a key point. This protrusion was called a salient and the convex shape it formed in the opposition line was referred to as a re-entrant. One such site, at the small Belgian town of Ypres, had formed after the first battle here in October 1914, with the line held by French, Canadian and British troops. In the late afternoon of 22nd April 1915, a strange smoke spread over the ground and poured into the French trenches along the northern part of the salient. Within 10 minutes around 6000 troops were dead, either their eyes and lungs destroyed by the chlorine gas or gunned down as they tried to scramble out of their trenches. The Germans though, had not expected the gas to be so effective and were not ready to exploit the huge gap they had created so late in the day. This enabled Canadian troops to cover the positions by urinating in cloths and holding them across their mouths to survive the worst effects of the gas. In a further series of battles, German gas attacks were stubbornly resisted by the Allies who surprised them with their determination to hold onto this position although by the end the salient had been reduced in size (see map) and Ypres was now within range of enemy artillery which would virtually flatten the town.

Both sides put in place major offensives during the spring and summer of 1915 along the Western Front, but all failed to make a breakthrough. There were shortages of ammunition and each time a breach was made a lack of communication meant reserves did not arrive quickly enough and the gap was closed. However, the first of Kitchener's Army, those which had volunteered in the previous year and had been training ever since, began arriving along the Western Front. As a result of failed offensives later in the year, the British commander Sir John French was replaced by Sir Douglas Haig. Haig believed that the enemy would have to be worn down by relentless attacks before any major push could be made.

Later Defences

The design of defences was always being updated and the Germans led the way in this science. British soldiers were often surprised when they captured German trenches to find how well built and equipped they were. The British, who thought that such permanent structures showed a lack of offensive spirit were slow to improve their own trench systems. However, in the last years of the war they established concrete factories to supply the material for the construction of bomb proof bunkers. Prefabricated pillboxes and machine gun posts were also imported from Britain to the front line.

The Germans established new defensive lines which were much wider and more complex than before. These defences could have gaps of up to a kilometre between them and consisted of carefully positioned concrete bunkers, machine gun posts and artillery positions as well as substantially built trenches, vast barbed wire entanglements and deeply dug telephone cables. They even created dummy positions to fool enemy airmen who flew over taking photographs. These defences were part of the reason why the often well planned Allied offensives made during 1916 and 1917 failed to make a breakthrough.

In Flanders fields the poppies blow
Between the crosses, row on row,
That mark our place; and in the sky
The larks, still bravely singing, fly
Scarce heard amid the guns below.

We are the Dead. Short days ago
We lived, felt dawn, saw sunset glow,
Loved and were loved, and now we lie,
In Flanders fields.

Take up our quarrel with the foe:
To you from failing hands we throw
The torch; be yours to hold it high.
If ye break faith with us who die
We shall not sleep, though poppies grow
In Flanders fields.

In Flanders Fields by the Canadian physician and soldier John Alexander McCrae was written from the point of view of the dead motivating the living to carry on the fight. Written in 1915, it came before the true horrors of trench warfare turned creative spirits to paint a darker, less romantic view of the war.

Chapter 3

Life in the Trench
Eating, Sleeping and Staying Alive

In late August 1914, the 17th Earl of Derby inspired the men of Liverpool to sign up for an exclusive battalion, in which he stated that, 'This should be a battalion of pals, a battalion in which friends from the same office will fight shoulder to shoulder for the honour of Britain and Liverpool.' Lord Kitchener promptly used the idea to encourage other towns, companies and sports teams to form their own 'pals' battalions. They would pass through training and on to the Western Front alongside their neighbours and colleagues. This seemingly successful method of recruiting had one major drawback; if they were all killed in action, a single community would be devastated by the loss of its young men.

In the East Lancashire town of Accrington, the mayor suggested forming such a group and within ten days over a thousand had signed up, more than half coming from the district, the others from neighbouring towns. This 11th Battalion, the Accrington Pals, formed part of the 31st Division of the 94th Brigade, which spent most of the following year training before embarking for Egypt where they still saw no action.

Lieutenant Colonel Arthur Wilmot Rickman was in command of the Accrington Pals on the fateful 1st July 1916. His report of the day's proceeding up until the point when he was injured by an explosion records the chronic problems with communications and the frustration of officers in the field as the full horror of what was happening became evident.

In February 1916, they were ordered to France and from April to June spent time in the trenches carrying out chores like making revetments and repairing barbed wire while suffering their first casualties as enemy artillery pounded their positions. This was all part of preparations for that year's major offensive around the river Somme, south of Bapaume.

Their part of the initial Somme attack was to take the hilltop fortress of Serre. At 7.30 am on 1st July, the Accrington Pals rose to charge at the German positions only to find that the artillery bombardments of the previous days had done little to damage the German defences. They were massacred by machine gun fire and rifle; as one observer stated, it was like, 'Swathes of cut corn at harvest time.' By 8.00 am the attack was over and of the 700 or so men from Accrington itself, 584 were recorded as dead, wounded or missing. When news broke back home in the town curtains remained shut and the church bells rang all day as the community of around 45,000 mourned the loss of such a huge proportion of its young men in just half an hour.

The experience of trench life, which was so tragically short for many of the Accrington Pals, was repeated in numerous other locations along the Western Front. A mass of men, cooped up in narrow, muddy ditches while the enemy shot guns, lobbed grenades, fired artillery or attacked them with poison gas or flamethrowers, made sectors of the front a horrendous place to be. Added to this was the constant threat of disease, rats and lice, while in winter frostbite, exposure and drowning claimed the lives of many.

In the opening half of 1916, despite no major battles in the British sector, there were still over 100,000 British casualties in the trenches. This meant that the chance of being killed on the Western Front was twice as high as it was in the Second World War, with only a 50 % likelihood of coming home alive and without a significant wound.

There could be great variations in the wartime experience, depending upon the location along the Western Front. There were sectors which saw little action from both sides. In some areas, an understanding existed between the Allied and Germans soldiers to avoid each other when patrolling, or to be able to carry out essential daily tasks without being attacked. In other parts, the war was relentless. This was especially the case for the British and Canadian troops trapped in the salient at Ypres, where they could be bombarded from three sides and from high positions overlooking the town. The local geology also affected how bearable trench life was. Some trenches were dug into well-drained soils and remained more habitable than the muddy, flooded ditches of the northern part of the front through Flanders.

British Army generals may have been insensitive to most of the problems which their men had to

Life in the front line trenches could be dangerous and depressing. There was a constant threat of being shot, hit by shrapnel, deafened by shell blasts or killed by poison gas or disease, not to mention being plagued by mud, rats and lice. Bad weather also caused frostbite, exposure and drowning when trenches flooded. Nor was it just the ordinary soldier who suffered as diseases and infestations were no respecters of rank. Officers tended to be the first to be killed when going over the top.

In this picture from 1916 on the Somme all seems quiet and peaceful. But the soldier on guard remains tense as he perches on the side of the trench, giving his comrades the sleep they desperately need. How many of them are there?

face in the trenches, as they sat safe in their bases miles back from the front line. They did however, understand about morale and keeping men sharp and they were obsessive about organisation. They arranged their forces so they would spend about a quarter of their time in the front or support trenches, another quarter back in the reserve line and the other half either in hospital or on rest, while many also got leave to go back to 'Blighty'. Hence a soldier might spend from as little as a day or so up to a couple of weeks at one time in the front line trenches, and while there he would probably have to stand on sentry duty for a couple of hours at a time on a rota. When they were not at the front, men would have to run supplies, repair trenches and carry out duties which still kept them within the firing range of enemy artillery. This situation was not the same for other Allied forces where there was not the depth of reserves. For them, time at the front might range from a month to an almost permanent occupation.

Commanders and officers had to organise the men under their command into this rotation of duties while also being expected to file daily reports, request supplies and list casualties. They also visited a new sector in daylight to familiarise themselves with its features and enemy positions before their men would move up into it later under darkness. A report would then be expected to be completed by the end of the next day on the state of defences, enemy positions and the quantity of ammunition. In effect, they had to file paperwork, order stores, check safety issues and comply with regulations just as we complain about today, except they were carrying it out in the most appalling conditions with the constant threat of death. Much of this bureaucracy though would go out the window when a major offensive loomed. Then men of all ranks had to get into position ready for the off.

Daily Routine

For the individual soldier on duty in the trenches, each day was planned and divided up for him into fairly regular routines, based around the fact that an attack or raid was most likely at dawn or dusk. Anyone who was sleeping was woken up around an hour before sunrise and joined the other men in manning the trench with bayonets fixed to their rifles in case of enemy action. This tedious 'stand to' with soldiers standing upon the fire-step and waiting for hours was often

A soldier on sentry duty, looking through a loop hole. Although tedious, this task was of such importance that men would be severely punished if they left their post or fell asleep.

termed the 'morning hate' by the men, and firing shells or a few rounds from a machine gun into No Man's Land would reduce the chance of surprise attack and help relieve the boredom. When the signal was given to end this 'stand to', men would have to check and clean their equipment and face an inspection from a Commanding Officer before they could have their breakfast. On most sections of the front, both sides observed a truce for a time while the wagons delivered the food and the soldiers ate, although if a Senior Officer found out about it this courteous practice would be quickly stopped.

34

When breakfast was completed, their NCO (Non-Commissioned Officer) would issue their tasks for the day, although with the constant threat from enemy snipers, shelling and observation balloons there was a limit as to what could be done. Most jobs involved the maintenance of the trench, for example, repairing collapsed walls and pumping out water after heavy rain. But there was also cleaning and preparing latrines and moving supplies. If they put their head up above the parapet for just a moment then enemy snipers would gun them down. In the breaks between tasks, soldiers could take a moment to brew a cup of tea (they often dug recesses in the walls to house a kettle), write a letter home or grab a short sleep. Soldiers in the British Army were also expected to look smart despite the horrendous conditions. There were no washing facilities for the ordinary soldier in the trenches, but they could shave with their helmet turned upside down to hold the water. Not everyone was involved with these tasks as snipers, machine gunners and stretcher bearers had to take it in turns to man their positions during daylight hours.

As dusk approached, the morning ritual of manning the fire step ready for a possible attack was repeated again, this time known as 'stand down'. When darkness enveloped them this finished and the trenches burst into life as more major tasks like digging new trenches, fetching supplies from rear lines, repairing defences and relieving front line troops took place. Despite the darkness, there was still a constant danger and a number of men had to stay on sentry duty, usually for no more than a couple of hours at a time so they would not fall asleep on the job.

German Barrage Fire at Night; Ypres 1915.

Night Patrols and Raids

Night time patrols and minor raids were carried out by small groups of soldiers, partly in order to keep men sharp and motivated, but also to gain more information about the enemy and dominate No Man's Land. Patrols would involve a few men crawling out across No Man's Land via a sap and listening in to the German line to try and find out information about planned attacks. It was a dangerous job as they would quickly come under fire if they were discovered and many clashed with enemy patrols trying to do the same thing to the Allies. When this happened, guns could not be used for fear that either side would hear

Volunteering and Conscription

After the initial enthusiasm to join the army, volunteers began to tail off during 1915 and various schemes and poster campaigns were run to try and inspire men to sign up. Music hall performers offered cash to the first man that night to come on stage and commit to the cause and stories were spread about German atrocities. However, with passions running high, civilian men who appeared to be of service age were sometimes attacked in public to the extent that those with a genuine reason not to sign up were given silver badges to protect them. Another problem for recruitment

officers was the poor state of health of the nation. The plight of the working classes and the slum conditions many of them lived in had largely been ignored by the ruling classes before the war, the result being that in 1915 only three out of every five enlisting were healthy enough for active service, and by 1917 it had fallen to only one in three. The army's limits on chest size and height were progressively lowered so that more fit young men could sign up.

Eventually, the government was forced to follow the lead of the other nations and introduce conscription. The Military Service Act was passed in January 1916 so that all single men between 18 and 41 years of age, and from May 1916 married men too, were eligible to be called up. They could appeal the decision on grounds of ill health, importance to the war effort at home or conscientious objection, and after six months around three quarters of a million men had done so. As a result of this and the poor health of recruits, only around 90,000 to 100,000 men were joining the army each month in the first half of that year and this fell away sometimes to as low as 30,000 a month. Despite these problems, the British Army, which had begun the war with a modest volunteer army, had by its end over five million men enlisted, roughly a quarter of the entire male population.

and start firing machine guns, so most times there would be a swift fight with fists and knuckle dusters before troops quickly returned to their respective trenches. Sometimes wire or string attached to old tin cans was laid out in front of the trenches to warn soldiers if the enemy tried to pass too close to their line.

Proper raids were far more ambitious and were carried out to take enemy prisoners, gain intelligence, steal supplies and keep the men occupied. They usually involved 20 to 30 soldiers who would cut their way through barbed wire emplacements, sometimes under the cover of an artillery barrage, and then attack a stretch of trench in order to snatch enemy soldiers, documents and booty. Pioneered by Canadian troops, they had become quite a well organised and planned activity by 1916, but their value, especially remembering the high cost of life when they went wrong, makes it debatable how useful they were.

The Risk of Injury and Death

Whatever daily routine the army put in place to keep soldiers' minds on the task in hand, the threat of death was ever present. The proportion of troops from Britain and her Dominions who were killed on the Western Front was around one in every eight, and over half the total number of soldiers became a casualty at some point during the conflict. It is estimated that over a third of those injuries were inflicted while serving in the trenches, most from exploding artillery shells of which a horrendous quantity by both sides were constantly fired.

Some soldiers were wounded by flying metal fragments (especially fatal if they were hit in the abdomen) or by the collapse of a trench due to the blast, while others were simply unlucky enough to be in the direct line of fire and stood no chance. The explosion could also kill a soldier due to concussion or from shock after the loss of blood from a wound. The most misunderstood symptom of prolonged exposure to shell blasts was shell shock, which could manifest itself through physical paralysis, a loss of sight and hearing, growths on the body, panic attacks and emotional breakdown. It affected thousands of soldiers and lingered with many long after the war had ended.

Taking a bullet was another common form of injury or death in the trenches, especially for newly arrived soldiers who were itching to look over the parapet and see into No Man's Land, only to be

Soldiers' Slang

It was inevitable that, with so many men from different classes and regions crammed into trenches words previously limited to a locality or military group should come into common use. Below are listed some of the more familiar which were either coined during the war or came into widespread use as a result of it.

Binge: A word for overindulging in drink, used originally in the north west of England.

Bint: From the Arabic word for a daughter.

Bivvy: From Bivouac, a temporary shelter for the night.

Blighty: A term used by English soldiers to describe Britain and home, from the Hindu word 'bilayati' meaning foreign land.

Boche: A British term for Germans, from the French word 'tête de boche' meaning an obstinate person.

Bumf: Shortened from 'Bum fodder', an 18th century term which was meant to describe toilet paper, but was used by soldiers as a derogatory term for official documents.

Cat Walk: A narrow path through fields only around 22cm wide (the length of a single brick).

Conk-out: To stop working, which was an unfortunate habit of some aircraft in the war.

Crummy: Itching caused by lice.

Cushy: Nice or easy, from the Hindu word 'Khush' meaning pleasant. Used by soldiers when they received a minor wound which permitted them a break from duty.

Dud: A shell which failed to explode, but which was also applied to anyone with a dubious character.

Flak: Anti aircraft fire which was formed from the first letters of the German words for a gun used for this purpose, '**fl**ieger **a**bwehr **k**anone'.

Glory Hole: A dug-out.

Gorblimey: A cockney term from 'God blind me', which was used to describe the service hat which slopped down over the head when the wire was removed from the top.

Mufti: Used by soldiers to describe civilian clothes, from the Arabic word meaning 'free'.

Plonk: Cheap wine, possibly derived from the French for white wine, 'vin blanc'.

Rumbled: To be found out, previous to the war used mainly in criminal circles.

Skipper: A word used by officers for a captain of a company, from the German or Dutch word 'schipper' meaning 'ship'.

Sweet Fanny Adams: This phrase meaning 'nothing at all' was a 19th century naval term for the poor tinned meat sailors had to eat, and came from the brutal nature of the murder in 1867 of 8 year old Fanny Adams.

Thingumyjig: Used in the war to describe a baffling new piece of equipment.

Tommy: A British soldier; from Tommy Atkins, the name which was often used by the army on specimen forms.

picked off in seconds by a sharp-eyed sniper. Trench periscopes were an essential piece of equipment as they allowed a view towards enemy trenches without putting their head above the parapet. Snipers were an ever present danger; they were heavily camouflaged and hard to see. They usually made their way out into No Man's Land at first light, hiding in saps, shell holes, ruined buildings and sometimes even being disguised as trees, and then would stay there all day just waiting for an opportunity.

Another sad end to life could come from the firing squad. This was a punishment for deserters, or even for those who had fallen asleep while on duty, which was why sentry duty was usually limited to a couple of hours only. Accidents were also a problem; tired soldiers with deadly equipment, prematurely exploding grenades, faulty ammunition and rifles jamming were all potential causes of injury and death.

Many died because of the poor conditions they had to endure through the seasons in the trenches. With heavy rain, water flooded into many of the trenches, trapping soldiers in thick mud and in extreme cases causing some to drown. The collapse of side walls due to the weather or artillery blasts often caught soldiers unawares and some could not be dug out in time to save their lives. In winter, exposure

was a real threat which claimed lives while frostbite could result in the loss of toes and fingers.

Perhaps the most feared weapon when it was first introduced by the Germans was poison gas (see page 67). There was chlorine gas which caused the tissue in the lungs to burn and soldiers to fall to the ground convulsing, choking and eventually dying. Phosgene was even more deadly, accounting for most gas-related fatalities during the war. The most notorious was mustard

A trench periscope which enabled men to look over the parapet without being shot. The soldier looked at the angled mirror at the bottom which reflected the image off the one at the top facing the enemy.

Shell Shock

Rarely before or since have so many soldiers been packed into such tightly confined spaces, and then bombarded by artillery shells which rained down on them at a rate of up to ten every minute. This ground shaking pounding of the trenches, ear splitting blasts and stress of warfare shook many of the soldiers trapped in the narrow ditches both physically and mentally. It manifested itself as panic, staring, a lack of reasoning, not being able to sleep or walk and in some cases soldiers simply wanting to run away. The first victims to suffer from what became known as shell shock were thought to have actual damage to the nervous system, however when it was attributed to a purely psychological reaction to the explosions there was little sympathy. Soldiers were branded cowards and a few were even shot as deserters. Towards the end of the war, officers were better trained to spot the early signs and medical facilities were laid on specifically for those with shell shock. However, some ten years after the war over 60,000 men were still recorded as suffering from its effects.

gas which, although it rarely killed, rendered soldiers incapacitated with horrific blisters on the skin, internal bleeding and the removal of the lining of the tubes leading to the mouth and nose.

Disease, Lice and Rats

As well as the enemy, there was a selection of other hostile elements which could make life in the trenches range from uncomfortable to deadly. With the appalling living conditions came the difficulties of maintaining basic hygiene, and disease became a major problem for the armies. Typhus, cholera and dysentery were all too common.

The most notable ailment was a fungal infection which thrived as soldiers' boots and socks remained damp for days at a time. Known as

trench foot, it could turn the limb red or blue and in the worst cases lead to gangrene, with the leg often requiring amputation. Improved supplies of socks and better drainage meant that this became less of a problem as the war progressed. With no chance of brushing their teeth, trench mouth became another common ailment, in which the gums became infected and developed painful ulcers.

Trench fever, although not usually fatal, was extremely painful and could incapacitate a soldier for a number of months. It was not established until the final year of the war that the culprits spreading this much feared ailment were lice.

Soldiers' clothing became riddled with the lice causing constant itching and infection from their excrement. Even if a uniform was regularly de-loused, the tiny eggs would often survive in the seams with new lice hatching within a few hours of putting the uniform back on.

One particular enemy affected soldiers more than most. With the mud and water lining the bottom of the trenches and a constant supply of human bodies, rats thrived. Soldiers of all sides were disgusted by them, especially as they could grow as large as cats by feasting upon the corpses lying in the mud, eating their eyes and inner parts. They would also eat the soldiers' rations, spread diseases and scamper over the faces of sleeping men, sometimes even taking a bite out of the living. There was not much that could be done about the problem, and although many were used as target practice or attacked with a bayonet or club, there were always more to replace them. A pair of rats could produce more than 800 offspring in a single year. Perhaps the only beneficial side effect of poison gas attacks was that it could clear an area of these much hated pests.

Soldiers were less concerned with it, but the most notable aspect of the trenches which struck new recruits was the awful smell. There were no washing facilities for the men; only a bath when they left front line duty after a number of weeks.

Trench foot was a common problem in the early years of the war when the trenches were often wet. In extreme cases, trench foot could lead to amputation.

Soldiers had to deal with a number of irritants while living in the trenches. These included lice, rats, flies, nits, frogs, slugs and beetles, some of which spread disease as well as caused injury. Rats were particularly hated by soldiers and were often killed as shown here, although this did little to reduce their numbers.

Battle of the Somme, 1st July to 18th November 1916

As the major offensives of 1915 drew to a close with the coming of winter, military leaders turned their attention to the following year with the French planning to attack the enemy line in the area around the River Somme with support from the British. However, in February 1916 the Germans launched an offensive against Verdun to the south and French divisions had to be sent there as they clung on to the town by the skin of their teeth. This meant that the planned Somme offensive would be a mainly British effort, with the intention now of relieving pressure on Verdun by drawing German forces away, being as important as any territorial gains. The preparation for the offensive was a massive operation with railways and roads built, new trenches and artillery positions dug, ammunition stored and telephone cables laid down. However, the Germans from their positions on high ground could see what was going on and began building deep concrete bunkers and new gun positions. They even knew it was going to begin on the 1st July.

As the Allied forces attacked on that fateful morning, two things quickly became clear. Firstly, that the bombardment of the previous week had done little damage to the German defences. Secondly, the British with a large proportion of inexperienced volunteers had not adapted to this modern war. They advanced slowly in straight lines and so were easily gunned down. The 1st July was the worst single day for the British Army with around 60,000 casualties,

of which 20,000 were fatal. The French moved more quickly in short bursts and then took cover, hence they suffered fewer injuries and made more progress. However, the problem of poor communication and failing to get reserves to hold territorial gains meant that progress was patchy and slow. General Sir Douglas Haig always intended this to be a wearing down process and as the battle dragged on over this 25-mile section of the front through the summer and autumn of 1916 the death toll grew. By the time it ended in mid November, the Allies had suffered over 600,000 casualties and nearly 150,000 killed, making it one of the bloodiest battles in history. Although it had done much to help relieve the pressure on Verdun, the territorial gains over four and a half months seemed small, with some targets set for the first day only reached in November.

Personal odour, especially from feet, was unavoidable. Added to this was the smell of cordite (the propellant used in rifle cartridges), chloride of lime (used as a disinfectant), rotting materials, cigarette smoke and remnants of poison gas. And then there were the latrines. With no toilet cleaners and overflowing waste, the stench could be so bad that soldiers often relieved themselves where they stood in the trenches, which only made things worse.

The most shocking aspect, however, was the odour from the dead bodies which lay in No Man's Land. There was rarely the opportunity to give the fallen a decent burial, even when the front pushed forward there was no time to stop and collect bodies. Sometimes there were brief truces to remove the dead from each side but in other sectors they might remain lying in the mud or dangling in barbed wire entrapments for months or even years. There could have been few more horrific reminders to the men when peeking out across No Man's Land than to see the rotting corpse of a colleague or friend, mutilated by rats and exposure to the elements.

British soldiers advance into No Man's Land at the Somme, 1916. The scene masks the fact that the men are walking in broad daylight towards a wall of barbed wire, exploding shells and machine gun fire from the German side. There is little protection other than a helmet. The bayonets fixed to the rifles could have been used for close combat by the few who made it into the enemy positions.

43

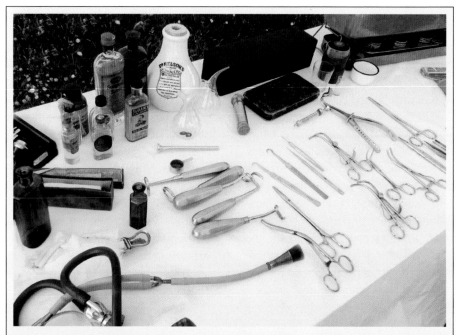

Royal Army Medical Corps (RAMC): despite the unsanitary conditions in the trenches and the sometimes primitive medical facilities and equipment which were available, the Royal Army Medical Corps managed to put back into the field something in the region of one and a half million men. Just behind the front line there would have been a regimental aid station where the injured could be patched up and either returned to action or sent further back for treatment. There would have been a few essential items like dressings, medicines, stretchers and a box containing brandy, cocoa or Bovril to comfort the injured.

Further back from this would have been an advance dressing station which had more room and equipment. Those that required surgery or rest were dispatched to a casualty clearing station. These were major establishments some ten to fifteen miles back. Although much of the equipment shown here is familiar to us today, other elements were not, with substances like opium and chloroform used to sedate patients and cocaine, lead and mercury used as medicines or lotions.

That said however, it is ironic that wars almost always aid the development of medicine. The vast number of wounded in the First World War allowed for the creation of specialist posts, for example, in anaesthesia and surgery, and the advances in most fields of medicine were dramatic.

The RAMC itself was not a fighting force but its members realised a man's chances of survival depended upon how quickly his wounds were treated, and they saw the full horror of the conflict. RAMC members won no fewer than eight Victoria Crosses.

Winter 1916-17

The winter of 1916-17 was the coldest in living memory. Sickness rates in the trenches increased and action was limited as the ground remained frozen solid until the following April. The German forces decided to construct a new defensive line along parts of the Western Front which would cut down the mileage to defend and allow extra divisions to be sent elsewhere. They withdrew to this new Hindenburg Line from March 1917, leaving a desert of burnt out buildings, destroyed defences and booby traps to greet the cautiously advancing Allies.

These seemingly pointless moves forward were the last straw for French troops. Mutiny spread through their forces which would restrict French fighting ability in 1917. The British had to start taking on conscripts to bolster their forces and these were less willing recruits for the fighting army.

The Germans also decided to reintroduce their submarine activity with the intention of destroying huge quantities of shipping and forcing Britain out of the war in late 1917. However, their activities only managed to anger a sleeping giant across the other side of the Atlantic, one who had already been angered by the German sinking of the *Lusitania* two years earlier. Now America had finally had enough and declared war on Germany on 6th April 1917. Although it would be nearly a year before they would have troops in action on the Western Front, there was finally a light at the end of the tunnel for the Allies.

Soldiers from an Army Cyclist Corps advancing through the gap formed by the German retreat back to the Hindenburg Line.

The bicycle had been an ideal vehicle for speedy and silent reconnaissance roles over many earlier campaigns. In trench warfare it was ineffective, but proved invaluable again once the static nature of the war changed in 1917/18.

Christmas 1914 and Unofficial Truces: Away from the busiest sectors of the Western Front unofficial truces between British and German troops were not uncommon early in the conflict. Sometimes they were called so that both sides could enter No Man's Land and retrieve their dead and wounded. The most famous of these truces took place in the days around Christmas 1914 at numerous points along the front. Soldiers began singing carols or shouting greetings at each other from their trenches until some plucked up the courage to step into No Man's Land. Gifts of food, alcohol or tobacco were exchanged, stories told, souvenirs taken and in a few locations a game of football took place. Despite several of the thousands who took part going before a court-martial, a similar attempt was tried by some in 1915. But attitudes towards the enemy were changing and only a few exchanges probably took place. By 1916, after regular poison gas attacks and the massacre at the Somme, any sort of truce seemed inappropriate with an enemy now viewed by many as sub human. The approach in many quiet sectors of 'live and let live', whereby troops deliberately aimed fire at precise points at regular times so the enemy could avoid being injured, probably continued throughout most of the war.

I've a little wet home in the trench,

Which the rain-storms continually drench;

Blue sky overhead,

Mud and clay for a bed,

And a stone that we use for a bench.

Bully beef and hard biscuits we chew;

Shells crackle and scare,

But no place can compare

With my little wet home in the trench.

Composed by Australian soldier and poet Tom Skeyhill and based on a popular song of the day. He was later blinded and wounded by a shell explosion and invalided home.

British magazines like *The War Illustrated* often sensationalised the conflict with imaginative pictures depicting events which might never have happened. The soldiers' own papers like the *Wipers Times* (named after the soldiers' slang for Ypres) were more satirical and humorous.

Chapter 4

Trench Warfare

Tactics, Weapons and Tanks

In the late summer of 1915, a visitor to the Yarborough Suite of the White Hart Hotel in Lincoln would have found the strange sight of a busy drawing office. Within were two men discussing various plans and producing designs before throwing them into the fireplace in disappointment. William Tritton was an expert in agricultural machinery and Major Walter Gordon Wilson a mechanical engineer. They had been appointed by a joint naval and military committee to develop an armoured tractor which could crush barbed wire emplacements and cross an enemy trench. Most of the work on these 'landships' (it was originally a naval project initiated by the First Lord of the Admiralty, Winston Churchill) had been completed. But the remaining problem was that the caterpillar tracks they were using would hang in mid-air when crossing a trench. However, on 22nd September the Admiralty received a telegram; the two engineers at the White Hart Hotel had cracked it. They had designed a new chain link system with flanges which would encircle the entire length of the vehicle. By Christmas that year the final prototype, called 'Big Willie',

William Tritton (left) and **Major Walter Gordon Wilson** (right) were responsible for much of the design of this new vehicle. After the war they were singled out and rewarded for their work.

had passed its tests successfully. The only problem which bothered Colonel Swinton, one of the first people to propose the idea, was that the name 'landships' might give away what they were planning to the enemy. He suggested that as the first experimental armoured vehicle looked like a large metal reservoir or cistern set on tracks, they should be called 'tanks'.

The habits of the 19th century were quickly wiped away and new tactics and weapons introduced in a desperate race to make the crucial breakthrough. In the space of just over four years, the way in which the infantry and artillery were used radically changed to meet the demands of trench warfare while improved guns, bombs, aircraft, tanks, flamethrowers and poison gas changed the face of warfare forever.

Tactics

Trench warfare came about because advances in weaponry were not matched by the same progress in mobility. German rapid-fire guns and new heavy artillery were aimed at the British, who were still moving around as if on a parade ground. Although tanks and aircraft which would later reverse this imbalance were available, their abilities were not fully appreciated and the tactics applicable to them still needed to be developed. Another reason why trench warfare developed was that once the Western Front formed a continuous line to the coast there were no flanks to get around the side of the enemy. This meant that most advances had to be made directly

Cavalry

Although many had warned that the days of cavalry as a fighting force were numbered, they were still seen as an important part of the British forces at the outbreak of war. The power of the charge was considered a valuable weapon and it was believed

that they could exploit gaps made in enemy defences with their speed. This proved tragically wrong along the Western Front as the horses were simply mown down by machine gun fire and artillery. However, as the area rapidly turned into a mud bath horses proved invaluable in moving artillery and supplies with hundreds of thousands brought from around Britain or imported from as far away as New Zealand. Horse feed was the single largest commodity imported into France during the conflict, and British veterinary hospitals which were established there, returned half a million animals back to health. The tank and armoured vehicles with caterpillar tracks eventually made it unnecessary to pluck these noble beasts from peaceful farm duties and throw them into the horror and torture of the war zone, as depicted in Michael Morpurgo's *War Horse*.

towards the enemy line. Soldiers and their commanders had been trained to expect a mobile war. As the conflict degenerated into a stalemate they had to develop a whole new approach to warfare.

During the time that the First World War unfolded, both sides felt that holding on to a position was of the utmost importance, while at the same time starving the opposition of resources and demoralising them with bombardments and raids. While the Germans built deeper and stronger defences to retain the large areas of Belgium and France they had acquired, the British commanders still sought a decisive battle which would break through the enemy trenches. This was the driving force behind General Douglas Haig's plans for offensives on the Somme and in Flanders, into which he placed human resources that continually floundered against a well-entrenched enemy. The result was a loss of life unparalleled in conventional warfare ever since.

The approach to major offensives in the early part of the war was to spend days bombarding the enemy's trenches with artillery in order to destroy the wire entanglements and as much of their main defence line as possible. Then the shelling would stop and the infantry soldiers would be sent over the top armed with a rifle and a bayonet fixed to the end (although only around 1 in 300 enemy soldiers were killed by bayonet). They would then move steadily towards the enemy in formation. Once the bombardment had ceased, the attacking troops had no protection as they struggled against enemy fire. It had always been assumed that an artillery barrage would easily smash an opponent's defences and it took some time for those in command to realise that this was not the case.

Invariably, the allies would find that only superficial damage had been caused by the shelling. They would be gunned down by an enemy well-protected in deep trenches and bunkers, who had been given ample warning of the impending attack by the bombardment. Another difficulty for allied attacking forces was that when a breakthrough was made, the necessary supplies and reserve troops could not be sent in support quickly enough. This was due to poor communications and the difficulties of moving across a muddy ground filled with shell holes. The Germans soon learnt that if they counter attacked promptly they could retake positions before reinforcements were brought up.

Changes were progressively introduced to resolve these problems. Artillery and infantry were eventually planned and

The Gallipoli Campaign 1915 to 1916

Away from the Western Front, trenches were rarely dug as the war on the Eastern Front and in the Middle East was more mobile. However, the campaign in Gallipoli, Turkey, (see map on page 85) was an exception and from the first landing there was stalemate, with the Allied Forces (including Australian and New Zealand Army Corps – ANZAC) facing even worse conditions than those for the troops in northern France.

With a static war on the Western Front, Britain and France sought to aid Russia by opening up a supply route through the Dardanelles, the Turkish Straits which linked the Aegean and Black Seas, and at the same time distract the Central

Powers, which since the 31st October 1914, had included the Ottoman Empire. The First Lord of the Admiralty, a young Winston Churchill, promoted an assault on the Gallipoli peninsula and British, French and Anzac forces landed on the 25th April 1915, but faced unexpected opposition and received heavy casualties.

'The actual fighting was the easiest of all,' remarked an Australian soldier wryly. He and his comrades faced these additional handicaps: the Turks held the higher ground and could snipe and shoot at targets below them at will. The climate of the peninsula was wet which meant easily flooded trenches; there were also very low temperatures in winter. Above all, the supply chain was erratic with unsuitable clothing, no fresh food and in particular a water supply that had to be rationed.

Unsurprisingly therefore, the Gallipoli Campaign was soon regarded as an embarrassing failure and soldiers were finally withdrawn in January 1916 with around 45,000 British, Australians and New Zealanders dead. The 25th April later became Anzac Day, a public holiday in Australia and New Zealand to commemorate the men lost in the war. Churchill also lost his job and spent time on the Western Front before returning to Government as Minister for Munitions, under David Lloyd George. The Prime Minister, Asquith, who also took some of the blame for the disaster, resigned in December 1916. This was a rare victory for the Turks as the faltering Ottoman Empire failed to hold onto its territory in the Middle East partly due to a British officer, T.E. Lawrence (Lawrence of Arabia) who helped inspire and organise an Arab Revolt against them.

controlled together. Big guns were used in shorter bursts so major offensives were less obviously advertised and aerial photography was used to pinpoint the areas that had been missed. A creeping barrage was formed with shells fired to drop in a line around 50 metres in front of the advancing soldiers and moved forward in short steps to keep the enemy stuck in their trenches. This gave some protection to the men from machine gun fire, although some were injured due to the close proximity of the explosions. Infantry attacks became more innovative and varied, with many made at night and involving soldiers crawling down saps and through gaps already cut in the enemy's barbed wire. Men now

Douglas Haig (1861-1928): Field Marshal Douglas Haig's command of the British forces during the First World War still splits opinions today. He replaced Sir John French as Commander in Chief in 1915 and was responsible for the planning of the Battle of the Somme and Passchendaele in which the army suffered some of its worst casualties. He has been criticised since for relentlessly throwing men into the mincing machine of German artillery and gunfire for worthless gains. Yet he also stood steadfast and unruffled by the immensity of his task; while others in similar positions came and went Haig stuck to his belief that the war would be won on the Western Front. His determination to finish the  job in 1918 against the wishes of politicians proved to be the correct course of action. He was a sound and patient General rather than an outstanding tactician, and was one of the few who appreciated that the war would be a long drawn out affair.

Haig made his name in its early stages when he mounted his steed to rally his troops in the face of defeat at the First Battle of Ypres. The manner in which the Germans gave up when they had been on the verge of victory possibly shaped Haig's belief that you should keep attacking until all avenues have been exhausted. He painted a confusing picture when it came to adapting to modern warfare, on the one hand welcoming the introduction of weapons like the tank and being open to new tactics to break the deadlock, yet in later years implying that he thought cavalry rather than artillery would still be key in future battles. Despite his apparent careless regard for the suffering of his troops, Haig spent much of his time after the conflict campaigning for their welfare and helped establish the British Legion (British railway workers in Argentina were instructed to name their new football team after him in 1918 and Club Atlético Douglas Haig still play in their league today). For all of his faults, many of which reflect the futility of this war rather than a personal incompetence, it should be remembered that he succeeded in his primary task; that of leading his country to victory.

moved forward as loose columns, winding their way across No Man's Land and using any available cover for protection. The first soldiers to get through enemy lines targeted selected strong points before the main body of men, who were in turn followed by reinforcements to hold onto any positions gained. Advances became less ambitious and would only be made when any previous gain had been reinforced. Light field guns were positioned where the attack started from and were used to provide cover while artillery and infantry were moved up, thus making counter attacks much harder for the Germans. By 1918, the way the war was fought and the weapons used were completely different to the outbreak four years earlier.

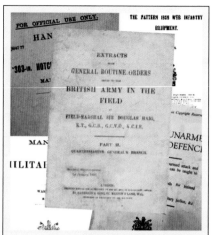

Tactics were published by the armies so that new ideas and changes could be passed down the chain of command. However, the enemy usually got their hands on the opposition's copies of these and each side roughly knew what the other one would be attempting, which only added to the deadlock.

Gas! GAS! Quick, boys! – An ecstasy of fumbling,
Fitting the clumsy helmets just in time;
But someone still was yelling out and stumbling,
And flound'ring like a man in fire or lime ...
Dim, through the misty panes and thick green light,
As under a green sea, I saw him drowning.
In all my dreams, before my helpless sight,
He plunges at me, guttering, choking, drowning.

From *Dulce et Decorum Est* by **Wilfred Owen**

By 1917 when this was composed a more realistic appraisal of the true horrors of the Western Front was being expressed by poets like Owen and Siegfried Sassoon. Despite being injured and sent home to recuperate in Britain, Owen returned to the front line but was killed just a week before the end of the war. A month previously he had captured a German machine gun post for which act of bravery he posthumously received the Military Cross.

Communications: A variety of methods were used including semaphore (holding flags in set positions to form a message), signal lamps (only worked one way or the enemy would see the message) and carrier pigeons (as in this example being released from a tank). The principal form used was the field telephone with wires run down the sides of trenches and later set below ground to avoid them being cut by exploding shells. However, they took time to lay down and connect up so were no good for a moving attacking force.

Wireless telegraphy was used by ships and aircraft throughout the war but this form of communication was still in its early days and the British commanders were reluctant to use it as there was no guarantee that the radio frequency was secure. In fact, British intelligence and signals corps spent most of the war listening in to enemy transmissions. They crucially intercepted the 1917 message in which the Germans promised Mexico that it could have back all the territory it had lost to the United States if it would join them against the Americans. This 'Zimmerman' telegram so enraged the United States that they finally declared war on Germany.

Weapons

Despite the industrial and technological might of the competing nations, their belief that it would be a short war meant that weapons and ammunition quickly began to run out once the sides became entrenched. For much of the first year of the war soldiers were required to improvise using clubs, maces, knives and even sharpened spades as weapons for close combat. Hand grenades made from old jam tins were another common sight in these early days. It was not until 1916 that supplies reached the required levels and new weapons more suited to trench warfare became available.

Artillery and Shells

First World War artillery pieces were the large guns or cannon which propelled explosive shells over great distances. They had evolved down the centuries with the most rapid development coming after the 1840s. Artillery guns now had rifled barrels, where the inside had slightly spiralled grooves which spun the projectile as it was shot out. This made it gyroscopically stable in flight, hence increasing range and accuracy. The shell usually had a copper driving band around it which engaged these grooves. Shells were also breech loaded whereby they were inserted into the rear of the

**The Third Battle of Ypres,
31st July to 10th November 1917:**
Messines Ridge to Passchendaele

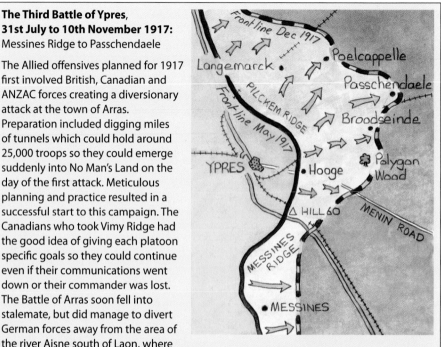

The Allied offensives planned for 1917 first involved British, Canadian and ANZAC forces creating a diversionary attack at the town of Arras. Preparation included digging miles of tunnels which could hold around 25,000 troops so they could emerge suddenly into No Man's Land on the day of the first attack. Meticulous planning and practice resulted in a successful start to this campaign. The Canadians who took Vimy Ridge had the good idea of giving each platoon specific goals so they could continue even if their communications went down or their commander was lost. The Battle of Arras soon fell into stalemate, but did manage to divert German forces away from the area of the river Aisne south of Laon, where the French Commander in Chief Robert Nivelle had launched a vast French offensive against the Germans, dug in on the Chemin des Dames ridge there. Nivelle was confident of victory in 48 hours with only 10,000 casualties. However, despite a few modest gains the attack was a disaster with no breakthrough and over 100,000 men dead or injured. Sections of the French Army disintegrated into mutiny and Nivelle was relieved of his post.

While the new French Commander in Chief, Philippe Pétain, tried to get the army back into shape the British went ahead with a planned offensive to take the high ground from the Germans to the south and east of Ypres. Preparation here involved tens of thousands of men building roads, more than 150 miles of railway being laid and tunnels dug under the ridge at Messines and loaded with powerful mines (see page 69, Mines and Mining). These would enable Allied forces to take the positions so attention could turn to objectives further east. Plans were finalised for British, Canadian and ANZAC forces to wear down the enemy and gain control of the strategic high ground. After initial failures during an unusually wet August, a more concentrated attack plan with shorter advances and improved communications between infantry, artillery and air support was found to be more successful. Gradually progress was made. The final phase of this campaign was the taking of the village of Passchendaele and the high ground around it, a long drawn-out battle with high casualties, only ending on 10th November.

The name Passchendaele is still remembered in the history books as a struggle of men over mud. It could not be described as a victory.

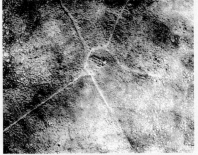

The 1917 offensives in Flanders
remain controversial today. Although
Haig argued that they occupied and
wore down the Germans while the
French were partially incapacitated,
they cost over 300,000 Allied casualties.
The millions of shells which were fired
devastated the landscape, turning it
into a shocking crater-filled sea of mud.
The pastoral village of Passchendaele,
pictured from the air before 1917 (top)
was virtually wiped off the map by the
end of the year (bottom).

absorbed the recoil (the sudden push back when the gun was fired) meaning that the artillery piece did not have to be re-aimed after each shot (hydro-pneumatic versions which used compressed air became standard by the end of the war as metal springs were prone to break after excessive use). The result of these and other technical changes extended the range and destructive power of cannon, with many different calibres and types of shell which could be used to attack an enemy installation, destroy defensive positions, demoralise enemy troops, or offer a protective shield to advancing soldiers. Such was the improvement in performance and their vital role in trench warfare that the percentage of soldiers killed by artillery in the mid-19th century, which had only been around 10 %, rose to nearer 60 % during the First World War.

Artillery was divided into two main categories. Field or foot were generally lighter, more mobile pieces which could be fired rapidly and with great accuracy. Heavy or siege artillery had a larger calibre and fired more destructive shells, they included some monster guns mounted on railway trucks. Within both of these categories there were two types of weapon. Firstly, there was a gun which generally had a longer barrel and accurately fired

gun with the crew positioned behind (rather than dropping the shell or projectile down the open muzzle). This resulted in more rapid firing. Sprung pistons mounted alongside the barrel called recuperators by the British were now fitted. These

a high velocity projectile, but at a maximum elevation of only 35 degrees. They were used for breaking up barbed wire entanglements or firing fragmentation shells above the surface. Secondly, there were howitzers, which fired a larger shell at a slower speed but with a greater elevation, usually more than 45 degrees, meaning that it dropped down into the ground. This made it more suitable for targeting trenches or bunkers. As the war progressed, new artillery was introduced.

The Arrival of Aircraft: The potential for aircraft in the theatre of war was not appreciated by many in 1914 but during the following four and a half years they demonstrated how they could bomb targets, take off from sea-going platforms, photograph enemy lines, and shoot each other down. Although we associate bombing raids with the Second World War they in fact started in 1915 with first Zeppelins and then in 1917 German Gotha aircraft. The first successful attack on London in June 1917 left over 160 dead, including 18 children killed by a bomb falling on a primary school.

On the Western Front their main role was reconnaissance which involved recording enemy defences, artillery, and troop movements at first by drawing them and later by means of aerial photography (as in this example of enemy trenches). Fighter planes were developed with greater manoeuvrability rather than speed to protect the reconnaissance planes and deprive the enemy of the chance to observe their forces. Air superiority over the trenches switched from one side to the other but during spring 1917, while the British were launching their attack on Arras, Manfred von Richthofen (better known as the Red Baron after his brightly coloured Albatross 111 biplane and later Fokker triplane) held the upper hand, with over 70 aircraft shot down by his squadron between the 4th to 8th April. Richthofen was a brilliant tactician rather than an aerobatic pilot and took most of his victims by flying down upon his enemy with the sun behind him, the devastating effect being that the life expectancy of a Royal Flying Corps pilot was only 18 hours during what became known as bloody April. (The Red Baron was finally shot down and killed on 21st April 1918).

Such was the importance of aircraft on the Western Front that much of the stalemate and resulting trench warfare can be attributed to the observations they made. In the final year of the war, the attacking and bombing potential of aircraft meant they were formed into a separate body on 1st April 1918, the Royal Air Force. With better communications and planning between aircraft, artillery and infantry, the commanders on the ground could now call upon planes to take out a defensive position or machine gun post which was holding up an advance.

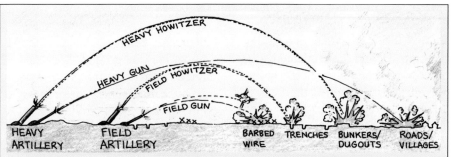

A **simplified diagram** showing the different types of artillery within a battery and the types of targets they might be aimed at. Field artillery was more mobile and usually positioned closer to the front line. Heavy guns and howitzers were set further back and could target defences behind the enemy line. Artillery would have to test its aim by 'registering' the piece before being used in action. When this was done earlier in the conflict, by firing at a target of a known distance away, it would alert the enemy as to its intentions and so later on artillery was registered behind the lines and then brought forward for firing.

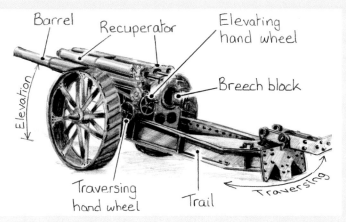

A **field gun with labels of its key parts**: In former times artillery had been aimed at targets which could usually be seen by the battery, or were fired en masse to obliterate an area. In the First World War indirect firing, where the target was out of sight, was increasingly used and perfected with an observer either concealed with a view of the target, or in an aircraft guiding the battery's aim. Careful calculation and adjustment was made so the rounds were fired with greater precision. The recuperator in this example dates from 1905 and was a hydro-spring unit (pistons housed within oil filled tubes to dampen the recoil while the springs absorbed the energy). They usually sat on top of the gun which made it vulnerable to damage from enemy fire, so it was often wrapped round with rope for extra protection. Later pneumatic compressed-air types had the device in a square tube below the barrel.

BL 6-inch 26cwt siege howitzer: The figures listed indicate the diameter of the barrel and the weight of it excluding the carriage; BL stands for breech loading. Confusingly, guns were categorized by the weight in pounds of the projectile but howitzers like this example were referred to by their calibre. The light or medium calibre guns, which were more mobile, were pulled by horses either of the Royal Horse Artillery or more commonly the Royal Field Artillery. The Royal Garrison Artillery was the force responsible for the new, less mobile,

heavy calibre guns and howitzers, usually positioned well behind the front line. This example which came into service in late 1915 could fire a shell over 10 km (6 miles). Larger 9.2" howitzers could fire a 130 kg shell just over 9 km (5 miles), but as the gun weighed nearly 15 tons it took over a day and half to dismantle before it could be moved. By the end of the war it has been estimated that the British Army had fired an astonishing 84 million rounds from their artillery pieces (that is an average of over 2000 rounds every hour).

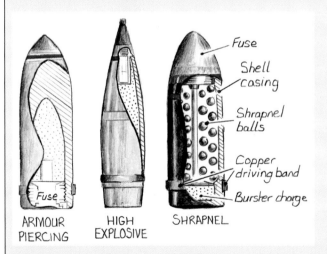

ARMOUR PIERCING   HIGH EXPLOSIVE   SHRAPNEL

Fuse
Shell casing
Shrapnel balls
Copper driving band
Burster charge
Fuse

Cut away views of three types of shell: The colour of the bands on the exterior indicated the contents and type. A chronic shortage of munitions quickly developed in the first year of the war, not least as a result of factory workers being killed due to problems with the design of some parts. This caused a scandal sufficient to bring the government down in 1915. David Lloyd George was appointed Munitions Minister to sort the problem out. Shrapnel shells, of which they had large stocks, were used to clear barbed wire but had to be very accurate in order to be effective. It was not until late 1916 that a new type of fuse was introduced which would reliably explode on the slightest contact with barbed wire. These enabled more effective high explosive shells to be used.

The new artillery brought together the attributes of both types and by the 1930s these had evolved into gun howitzers.

In the First World War, guns and howitzers fired shells, which were hollow metal projectiles. These were designed to deliver their explosive payload by either ejecting it out of the nose or base or by bursting. There was a wide range of types and sizes with a variety of loads depending upon the target and their position. Shrapnel shells were nose ejected and had a fuse which ignited a small charge when they were dropping down towards the target. This forced the nose to blow out, along with the metal balls inside. These would form a narrow, cone-shaped spread which was designed to injure soldiers in open spaces. The majority of British ammunition was of this type at the opening of the war. However, as soon as the trenches were dug they proved relatively ineffective so in response to this high explosive shells were developed. These fragmented into lethal shards, flying off in all directions, and proved more suitable for trench warfare (shrapnel is often incorrectly used to refer to these metal fragments from a bursting shell). Armour piercing shells were later introduced to counter the threat from tanks. They were achieved by making the shell casing thicker towards the nose, although they often had a soft tip so the projectile did not shatter on impact (for gas shells see page 67, Poison Gas).

Gunpowder and lyddite were still used in shells but a new high explosive called Amatol, which was a mix of ammonium nitrate and trinitrotoluene (TNT for short although the British usually called it trotyl), became increasingly standard.

For the projectile to be fired it needed a fuse, a propellant and a primer. These components along with the shell, constituted a round. The fuse was the device that triggered the shell to explode and could either be timed to go off in flight or when it hit the target (percussion). Most were fitted into the nose of the shell and could be selected to suit the nature of the target and distance. The propellant was a low explosive, that is one which burns and releases gas to propel the projectile rather than high explosive which generates supersonic shock waves, and is held in cloth bags to form what is termed the cartridge. Cordite was used in the First World War either in a fixed quantity for guns so it would reach its maximum range (a full service charge) or with rings around a central core in a howitzer so the quantity could be adjusted to decrease or increase the charge (the amount of propellant required to fire the projectile the necessary distance). The primer which ignited the propellant could be part of the cartridge or be built into the breech block at the rear end of the barrel. In quick firing guns all components could be contained in a single shell called a fixed round to speed up loading.

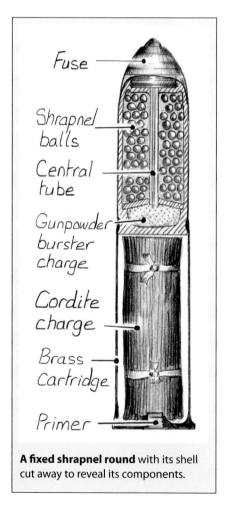

Fuse

Shrapnel balls

Central tube

Gunpowder burster charge

Cordite charge

Brass Cartridge

Primer

A fixed shrapnel round with its shell cut away to reveal its components.

Mortars and Grenades

Another type of artillery were mortars which fired a bomb at a steeper angle of elevation than a howitzer. At the beginning of the war the British Army had virtually none of this type, as a mobile conflict in open countryside had been predicted and mortars were not expected to be of any use in this situation. However, as soon as the Western Front became established the Germans, who had seen the advantage of these weapons in trench warfare after studying the 1905 Russian-Japanese conflict, had already put a number of mortars into production. Because of the steep angle they could be fired at, and their more compact size, they could be positioned in a trench to fire bombs into an enemy's position or destroy barbed wire obstacles very effectively. Simple lightweight versions could also fire more rapidly. The British officers who were on the receiving end quickly realised their potential and requested that the army supply something similar. The first attempts were rather improvised, the priority for production was on guns, howitzers and their ammunition. Some types referred to as bomb throwers were merely elaborate catapults. What the army really needed was a simple design which could be manufactured at smaller, less specialised factories and workshops that were not already involved in larger artillery work. The 2" medium trench mortar and stokes mortar, both designed in 1915 and put into production later that year, fulfilled this role and were widely used in the trenches (only around 500 mortars were fired in 1914 compared with over 6,000,000 by 1916). These were portable weapons which could be used by the infantry (heavy mortars were usually the responsibility of the Royal Field Artillery) and could be fired from within the trenches by inserting or dropping the bomb down the barrel (muzzle loading), with some models able to fire up to 25 times per minute.

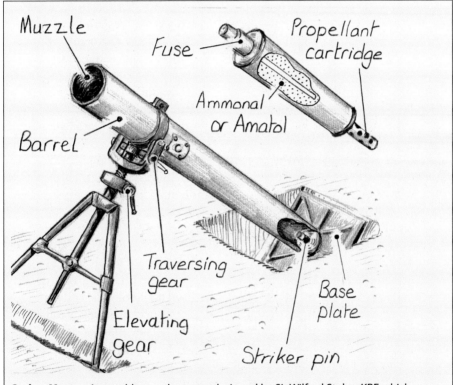

Stokes Mortar: A portable trench mortar designed by Sir Wilfred Stokes KBE which was set up on a base plate to absorb the recoil with front legs which varied the angle of elevation. The most common type of bomb used looked a bit like a rolling pin (top right) and was dropped down the barrel, hitting the firing pin at the bottom which ignited the propellant and shot it out. This meant that another one could be quickly inserted, enabling rapid fire. The range to the target could be simply adjusted by altering the angle of the barrel and the number of rings of propellant in each bomb.

Like mortars, hand grenades were ideal for trench warfare as they could be thrown at close quarters towards enemy soldiers or into trenches, where they would explode, sending lethal metal fragments flying in all directions. Unfortunately, like mortars, the British had hardly any stocks of them at the opening of the war. The Germans were better prepared and had numerous types with a metal case and a wooden handle to make it easier to throw accurately over a distance. A British version had been produced in limited numbers, however it proved dangerous as it was too easy to hit their own trench when thrown. As a result, improvised versions with the explosive and fuse fitted inside empty jam tins from soldiers' rations were used throughout 1915, until mass-produced types were finally available in quantity. The most notable of these was the familiar Mills grenade, made from a cast iron shell with a detonator ignited a set time after releasing the safety pin. These were an efficient and destructive device and became the primary weapon for use in the trenches when used at close quarters. Mechanical grenade throwing machines were largely replaced by rifle grenades later in the war. These had a wooden stick inserted into the muzzle of the rifle and were shot out by a blank round.

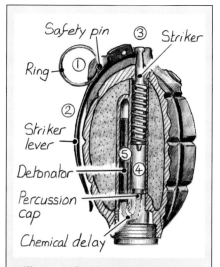

Mills Grenade: The Mills grenade was a simple, robust and reliable design which was easy to manufacture. Its distinctive cast metal case had grooves across it to make it easier to grip. To use it the soldier held the striker lever and grenade tightly so the safety pin (1) could be pulled out and then thrown towards the target. Once gone, the striker lever (2) flew loose releasing the striker (3) which was rammed downwards by the spring. This hit the percussion cap (4) creating a spark which was carried down the chemical delay for a set time before it reached the detonator (5) and ignited the surrounding reservoir of explosive material, shattering the case around four seconds after it was released. It is estimated that over 70 million various types of grenade had been thrown by the end of the war.

Medium Mortar: The distinctive shape of the projectile used in this mortar, with a football-size cast iron bomb and a stick which was inserted down the barrel, gave the weapon the nickname of 'toffee apple' or 'plum pudding' mortar. It was mass-produced from August 1915 in railway and agricultural machinery workshops and was efficient at clearing barbed wire entanglements, although its limited range meant it could only be used where No Man's Land was relatively narrow.

Rifles and Bayonets

The infantryman's standard weapon was the Lee Enfield bolt action rifle. This gave a variable shooting range, close being up to 550 metres (600 yards), effective 550-1300 metres (600-1400 yards), long 1300-1800 metres (1400-2000 yards) and distant 1800-2500 metres (2000-2800 yards). It was issued along with an M1907 bayonet, a 17 inch blade and handle which attached to the underside of the muzzle for charging at close quarters, but could be used as a weapon or tool in its own right.

The rifle fired 0.303 inch cartridges which resembled mini shells, with a propellant and percussion cap in the base which would fire the top section (the bullet) out of the barrel. These components within a full metal jacket constituted a 'round'. To use the rifle, the bolt was pulled back so the 'spent' round was ejected and the magazine would push up another round. The bolt was then pushed back so it engaged in the barrel and when the trigger was pulled so the firing pin hit the percussion cap in its base, thus igniting the propellant. The bullet would be shot out of the cartridge, expanding slightly so it engaged in the barrel's rifling and forcing it to spin in flight for increased accuracy.

Rifles and shotguns were often adapted for individual use during the war, snipers added telescopic sights and some soldiers used sawn off shotguns for trench raids. Hand guns were issued to officers, military police, machine gun operators, aircraft and tank personnel, the standard issue in the British Army being the Webley Mk IV revolver. It was found to be reliable even in the muddy conditions of Flanders, although the reputation of the German Luger meant that some officers preferred to use these when they were captured from the enemy. ANZAC troops at Gallipoli used a periscope rifle which could be fired without the soldiers having to raise their heads above the top of the trench, but its lack of accuracy meant that it was mainly used when the lines were as close as 50 metres.

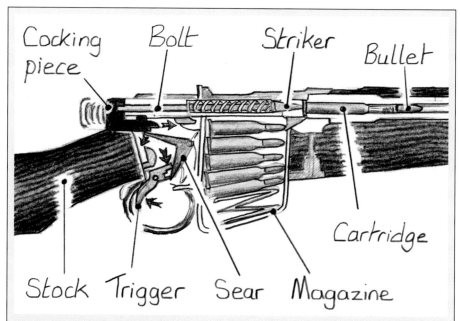

Short magazine Lee Enfield rifle: A cut away view of the workings of this standard issue British rifle (the bolt system was designed by James Paris Lee and the barrel rifling was adapted from an earlier model at the Royal Small Arms Factory in Enfield hence the name Lee Enfield). It was reliable and simple to use with relatively rapid fire. Its fast operating bolt action could be used without taking the eye away from the sights, enabling 15-20 aimed shots to be made every minute. It was issued along with an M1907 bayonet, a 17 inch blade and handle which attached to the underside of the muzzle but could be used as a weapon or tool in its own right.

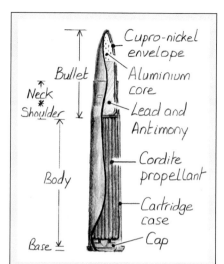

0.303 inch cartridge: When the rifle's firing pin hit the percussion cap at the bottom it ignited the cordite propellant firing the bullet out of the barrel. The tip had a lightweight interior so that when it hit a target the heavy base caused it to veer to one side creating a more severe wound. A Lee Enfield could fire this bullet at around 740 metres per second and was able to shatter a brick or penetrate a half inch sheet of steel at a certain range.

Machine Guns

Machine guns were one of the most lethal weapons of the First World War, most notably at the Battle of the Somme where soldiers coming forward or caught in barbed wire entanglements were mown down by their rapid fire. Although the machine gun had been around for many decades, it was not until 1884 that Sir Hiram Maxim invented one which was self powered rather than turned by a handle, using the energy from the recoil to load the next bullet. The Maxim company was bought out by Vickers in 1896. They improved the design by making it lighter and simplifying the action, their new weapon being adopted by the British Army in 1912. However, the Germans were far more appreciative of the potential of the machine gun and had three times as many per battalion than the British. It was

Helmets: Soldiers went into the First World War with just a cloth cap so when they became trench-bound head wounds from shell fragments quickly escalated. It was not until late in 1915 that a helmet, designed by John L. Brodie and made by pressing out a single sheet of steel was adopted by the army, although at first they were in short supply and only used by those on the front line. Note the rifle grenades on the barrels being held by these soldiers wearing Brodie helmets.

not until the high cost of the Vickers was lowered that it became more widely available. Part of the army's reluctance in adopting it was that it was heavy, took time to set up and required a team of up to eight men to carry the weapon and ammunition around. This made it of limited use for the predicted fast moving open warfare. However, once the Western Front became established these heavy machine guns came into their own. Positions were dug where they could cover the area in front of the trenches while later techniques were developed to provide indirect fire (firing over an obstruction like a hill with the bullets plunging down onto the enemy beyond) where it could be effective from up to 4000 metres. The Machine Gun Corps was established in October 1915 so they could be better utilised and soldiers trained in their use while the lighter Lewis gun provided a more mobile alternative to the Vickers.

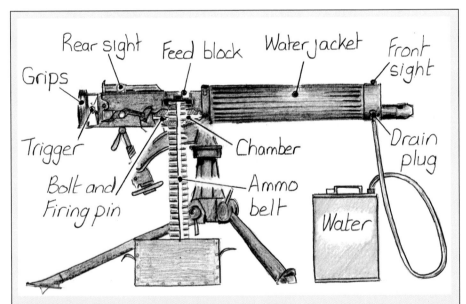

Vickers Gun: A diagram of a Vickers .303 British machine gun with labels of its key parts. The cartridges were fed into its mechanism on a belt with the expended gas from the previous shot being used to push the bolt back, expel the spent cartridge and reload the next.
This efficient self-powered system could be used at incredible speeds of up to 450 rounds per minute with an effective range of around 2000 metres (direct fire). The gun gained a reputation for excellent reliability and robustness, remaining in service until the 1960s.
The only problem with these machines was the heat generated by rapid firing so a water cooling jacket was wrapped around the barrel and connected to a supply of water in a can.

Lewis light machine gun: The Lewis gun was invented by Isaac Newton Lewis in 1911 but because he had issues with the chief of the American ordnance department he had to bring his design to Europe where it was made under licence by the Birmingham Small Arms Company. The British Army adopted this lighter weapon in 1915; the speed with which it could be manufactured and its versatility resulted in nearly 50,000 being produced during the war. The cartridges were fed into its mechanism via a circular magazine holding up to 97 rounds mounted on top, with the firing sequence powered by the gas expended by the previous cartridge. The blast from the muzzle was used to draw fresh air back into the mechanism to keep it cool. This effective system, along with its light weight, meant it could be fired by a soldier with or without a swivel mount and was ideal as a mounted weapon on aeroplanes.

Poison Gas

The most feared weapon during the First World War was poison gas. Its first large scale use on the Western Front, and its most devastating, was at the Second Battle of Ypres when the Germans released over 150 tons of chlorine gas from thousands of cylinders, relying upon the wind to blow it over the French and Algerian troops to create a massive gap in the front line. However, troops quickly realised that standing still upon the fire step (the gas clung to the ground) and putting a damp cloth across their mouth reduced its effects. When news of this attack reached the public, *Daily Mail* readers produced hundreds of thousands of cotton pads only for it to be discovered that when wet they actually suffocated the wearer with a number of soldiers dying as a result. Fatalities from gas attacks reduced as men were issued with a smoke helmet. This was based on a design from a serving Canadian doctor Cluny Macpherson. It was a cloth bag with eye pieces and a single exhaling tube which could be impregnated with chemicals to neutralise the effects of the gas. By 1916, a new type was introduced which had a tube connecting the mask to a filter; and this small box respirator soon became standard issue to all men. Masks were also developed for the horses and dogs which were used on the Western Front.

Although the Allies were quick to condemn the use of gas as unsporting, they were equally rapid in the development of their own types. The first notable use by the British though was a disaster, as the wind that began blowing it towards the enemy changed direction and in some places blew the gas back towards their own troops. In addition, there were further British casualties when the gas cylinders they had kept in reserve were hit by enemy fire and released the gas behind the lines. Artillery shells filled with poison gas were soon developed and became a more predictable method of releasing the deadly chemicals at the enemy. However, with masks and training it rarely had a devastating effect upon defenders along the Western Front, with around 1 in 25 deaths due to it. Gas became just another part of the bombardment preceding an attack.

Other gases were also developed; the most fatal being phosgene which was colourless and hence harder to detect,

although its effects might not become apparent until a day after inhalation so soldiers could still fight on. Phosgene was first used in December 1915 by the Germans and although produced in smaller quantities than chlorine, it accounted for nearly six out of every seven deaths by gas during the war. Dichlorethylsulphide, called 'Hun Stuff' by the soldiers, but better known as mustard gas was widely used towards the end of the war. This was a blistering agent rather than a poison and caused large and extremely painful fluid filled blisters over the skin; it also damaged eyes and created breathing difficulties. It formed a liquid over the ground where it fell which could remain active for weeks afterwards.

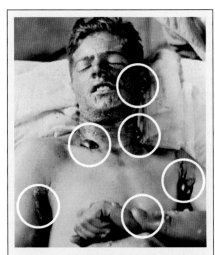

A soldier suffering with blisters and burns (highlighted by the rings) from mustard gas exposure.

Flamethrowers:
A simplified diagram showing the principal of how a flamethrower works. The pressurized gas forces the fuel out which is then ignited as it leaves the lance creating a jet of flame and smoke up to 20 metres long. The first practical modern type was invented by Richard Fiedler in

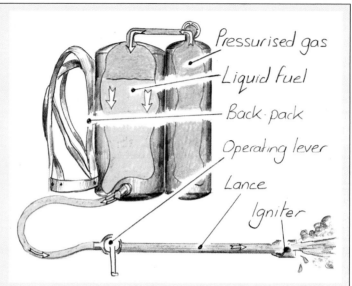

Pressurised gas

Liquid fuel

Back-pack

Operating lever

Lance

Igniter

1901 with a portable version being adopted by the German Army prior to the war. Its first major use on the Western Front was against the British at Hooge in July 1915 but despite this successful attack there were limitations to its use which meant it was only effective at close quarters. The main problem was that the flames and smoke immediately attracted the enemy's attention and the operators were usually showered with a hail of bullets or were picked off by snipers. They also had to carry the heavy equipment around with the risk that it might blow up at any time and they knew that if they were caught they would be executed, such was the contempt for the weapon. Although the Allies experimented with them, they remained principally a German weapon .

Mines and Mining: One of the most incredible but largely forgotten features of the war were the tunnels dug to gain a strategic position or to explode mines in order to destroy enemy defences. They were dug by the Royal Engineers, soldiers who had been civilian miners and other Allied forces. They risked their lives not only from the dangers involved in mining but also from Germans digging tunnels of their own to intercept them. In the construction of tunnels at Arras in 1917, over 40 New Zealanders were killed and another 150 injured by German counter mining. The most successful example of tunnelling occurred in the area around Hill 60 as a prelude to the Third Battle of Ypres that year, when the British loaded tunnels with powerful mines containing around 1,000,000 lb of explosives. On 7th June at 3:10 am, 19 were successfully detonated in the largest man made explosion ever known at that date (it was heard back in Britain) killing thousands of German soldiers almost instantly as the top was blown off the ridge and leaving huge craters up to 80 metres (260 ft) in diameter. These are now filled with water and are still visible on satellite images.

Tanks

No sooner had the demonstrations of Tritton's and Wilson's prototype been made than orders were placed and 60 Mark 1s were being shipped out to take part in the Somme offensive, with only a vague plan as to how they would be used. There was little ground testing and the crews were not fully trained. As a result, when they trundled into battle in September 1916, 17 broke down before even reaching the front line. Those which made it through proved themselves useful and Haig was so impressed that he made a huge order for more of them. However, the element of surprise had been lost, the Germans were able to study them and devise tactics and weapons to counter their threat, hence when they were used in early 1917 they were not successful. It was not until Mark IV tanks arrived later in the year and new tactics for their use were employed that they became more effective.

These early tanks had their caterpillar tracks wrapped around wheels to form a distinctive rhomboid shape when viewed from the side,

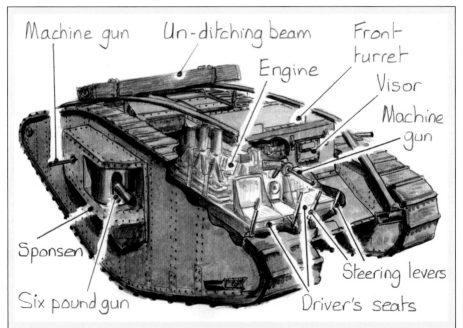

Machine gun Un-ditching beam Front turret Engine Visor Machine gun Sponsen Six pound gun Steering levers Driver's seats

A Mark IV Male tank with a cut-away showing part of the cramped interior the crew of eight had to work within. It had two 6 lb guns with shortened barrels at the front of each side turret; the female variant only had machine guns.

designed specifically to cross the crater and trench-filled landscape of the Western Front. The Mark IV was the most numerous type, used from summer 1917 up until the end of the war. It was only 8 metres long but weighed nearly 30 tons, partly due to its armour plating which was up to 12 mm thick. Inside was a large 6 cylinder petrol engine which generated around 100 bhp, meaning that its huge bulk could only move at around 4 mph with a range limited to 30 miles due to the high fuel consumption. The tanks were designated as either male, which had a 6 pound artillery gun side and three machine guns, or female which was lighter with just five machine guns. These weapons were positioned to the sides within a pair of projecting side-turrets and a single machine gun at the front. Although the Mark IV was similar to the earlier Mark I (Mk II and III were used for training and never served on the front) it had a number of additions, most notably the shortening of the gun barrels to the sides. The earlier tanks often got grounded in the mud when crossing a trench. A wooden beam was lashed to the back that could be chained to the front of the tracks if the tank got stuck, where it would be drawn under giving it extra grip, like snow chains on a car tyre. A large bundle of brushwood was also carried on the front, to drop into deep trenches to make them easier to cross.

These huge mechanical beasts were manned by a crew of eight, a commander with seven others operating the guns, the driving and steering was done via a series of levers (the later Mark V could be controlled by one person). The conditions the crew had to work in were simply appalling. Not only were they under constant risk of being blasted by artillery and gunfire or incinerated by grenades if they got grounded, but also the fumes and heat from the engine and weapons meant that the interior was toxic with a temperature often as high as 50 °C. With little in the way of ventilation it was not unusual for crews to be rendered unconscious while operating them.

The noise inside was such that the men had to communicate via hand signals. There was added danger too for those who had to go outside and attach the unditching beam or release the bundle of brushwood while in the middle of enemy territory. Needless to say, the life expectancy of the men in the Tank Corps was extremely low. In 1918, when the Germans had once again worked out how to destroy them, it only got worse and there were merely a handful of tanks left operational by the time the war ended.

A Mark 1 tank with rear steering wheels, a vulnerable feature which was quickly dropped from the design. These first tanks could only manage 2-3 mph with poor armaments, limited gun fire and communications restricted to semaphore or even carrier pigeon. The press and public however were captivated, believing it would win the war for Britain and they snapped up toy tanks and memorabilia.

Battle of Cambrai, 20th November to 7th December 1917: One final offensive was planned for late 1917 in which new tactics involving close co-operation between artillery and infantry were to be tried out. A section of the German front line near the French town of Cambrai, known to be well-fortified, was the chosen site and tanks were to be used in large numbers. However, this time they were divided into groups of three which would form an arrow, with the soldiers following on foot behind. Artillery could now register their guns on enemy targets by using sound ranging and increase the chance of surprise. The operation began on the 20th November with a short but intense artillery attack followed by a creeping barrage under which the tanks and infantry advanced, making great inroads into German territory. However, the usual problems with communications and the inability to bring reserves up quickly meant that the Germans were able to call in reinforcements and counter-attack with most of the land gained lost after a couple of weeks of fighting. The battle had shown the effectiveness of the new tactics and to some degree the value of the tank, at least in the initial drive to cross barbed wire and disable machine gun posts. At the same time it had emphasised to the Germans the great measures they would have to take to defeat the threat of the tank and future Allied attacks, ones which they were increasingly not in a position to do.

The blockade of German ports had also begun to have an effect and supplies at home and on the Western Front were running short. Some Germans already realised that the following year would be make or break for them, not only because of dwindling armaments and food but also because the Americans would be ready by 1918. However, a successful offensive alongside the Austrians had crippled the Italian Army, forcing Britain and France to send reinforcements, which weakened their ability to attack on the Western Front. At the same time, the Russians had pulled out of the war as their country disintegrated into revolution and now the German forces from the Eastern Front could reinforce those in the west so a major German offensive finally to win the war for the Central Powers could be planned for spring 1918.

Going Home

1918 and the Aftermath of War

Henry Tandey was the most decorated British private during the First World War. He had fought at the First Battle of Ypres, the Somme and Passchendaele, twice being seriously wounded but each time returning to service. He was awarded the Distinguished Conduct Medal when he and two colleagues bombed a trench which was holding up an advance and took 20 prisoners, and then the Military Medal after leading a similar daring raid two weeks later. He received the highest and most prestigious award, the Victoria Cross, when on the 28th September 1918 he crawled forward to locate and then help take out a German machine gun post, restored a vital bridge crossing and bayonet charged the enemy despite being wounded.

On the German side of the Western Front was a lance-corporal, well liked by his fellow soldiers who called him 'Adi'. But despite his apparent bravery and willingness to take on the most hazardous of tasks, he showed little initiative to lead men and be promoted beyond his lowly rank. He was a runner, part of a team of soldiers who every

Henry and Adi - two soldiers on opposing sides of the Western Front but whose futures would take extremely different paths.

evening would dash across the battle grounds under a hail of bullets or exploding shells to deliver messages to headquarters. He excelled in these duties to such an extent that he was awarded the Iron Cross First Class in August 1918.

These two unassuming characters on opposing sides of the war were to meet for a brief moment when the German, clearly wounded, stumbled into the British soldier's line of fire. Showing remarkable compassion, Tandey noticed that Adi was wounded and signalled to him to move on out of the way. The German, expecting that his end had come, gratefully acknowledged this and hobbled away. The two men would never meet again. It was not until nearly 20 years later that Henry Tandey, who had left the Army in 1926 and was now working at a car factory in Coventry, was contacted by the Prime Minister, Neville Chamberlain. Chamberlain had just returned from the ill-fated appeasement trip to Germany where he had met a certain gentleman who wished to pass on his gratitude to Tandey for not killing him on that fateful day. It turned out that Adi had remembered the incident so clearly he had even hung a painting on his wall showing Tandey carrying a wounded colleague. However, Henry Tandey was in for a shock when Chamberlain told him the full name of the man he had saved was Adolf Hitler.

The accuracy of this story, as with much which surrounds the Nazi leader, is debatable. However, it does emphasise the fact that despite the extraordinary bravery of soldiers on both sides, the long term legacy from the First World War would not just come from the events on the battlefields but from the decisions and events which happened in its aftermath. Trench warfare would leave an indelible mark on those who returned from the Western Front. However, it would be the way in which the war leaders and politicians divided up the spoils but failed to work together in a reconciliation which would cause future problems and create a situation in which Adolf Hitler could rise to power.

The End of the Stalemate

With additional forces now released from the Eastern Front, Germany planned their spring offensive in 1918 using specialised storm trooper units made up of the fittest and youngest soldiers. They were to make rapid attacks, targeting the weakest parts in the line and then pushing on past any points of stubborn resistance, leaving a following wave of infantry soldiers to deal with them. It was not a new idea, all sides had developed similar tactics, but this would be the first effective use of it on a large scale. On 21st March, a short but intense artillery and gas attack was launched and the storm troopers went in against the British, forcing their way through to avoid getting bogged down in prolonged combat, while a second wave with mortars, grenades and flamethrowers took on the strong points left behind. This was the first of four attacks launched during the spring of 1918, each making impressive initial gains and one getting within 60 miles of Paris. The stalemate of trench warfare had finally been broken.

There were problems though with the German Spring Offensive. They

The Spring Offensive 1918

The British knew that the Germans were planning an attack and had restructured their defences. They were now spread over a deeper area with three zones rather than just lines. There was a forward zone which would be lightly defended by patrols, machine gunners and snipers, a central battle zone where an offensive was intended to be held up by serious counter attack, and a rear zone in which reserves could be placed.

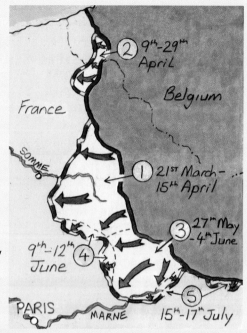

The Germans attacked on 21st March with the heaviest bombardment of the war upon a 40 mile stretch of British held lines south of Arras. Over 3,500,000 shells were fired in five hours, with heavy guns targeting headquarters, artillery positions, communications and supply lines at the rear while gas and mortars were fired at the front. Storm troopers burst through in the confusion and made good progress over the following weeks pushing well into France, until the operation ground to a halt and was finally called off on 5th April.

For all their gains the Germans had failed to take any of their strategic targets and had suffered around a quarter of a million casualties, mainly to their irreplaceable storm troopers. The map shows the five phases of attack by the Germans and the furthest extent that they had reached by July 1918.

had struck against the strongest part of the line rather than the weakest, and so faced stiff resistance. Also their forces were slowed down by having to cross rivers and canals or pass through woodland and urban areas. The storm troopers themselves were also suffering. Unlike the Allies, they were not rotated and soon became exhausted. An influenza epidemic took out many of their number while their capture of Allied stores made them realise that they had been lied to about the success of their U-boat campaign. Attacks petered out as the starving soldiers feasted themselves on food and alcohol.

As so often happened during the First World War, the opposition obtained pamphlets outlining new tactics before an attack had begun and could therefore work out counter measures. In this case, the French had devised new methods of defence which drew the Germans into attacking gaps they had left open, and in which they could then make surprise counter-attacks. This plan was backed up by American troops who by May were arriving in large numbers, and resulted in the failure of the two final attempts by the Germans at a decisive breakthrough. By mid July, after the French had counter-attacked at the Second Battle of the Marne, the Germans were exhausted and demoralised. They had suffered around 800,000 casualties since March. The tide was about to turn for the last time.

The Closing Months of the War

The Allies, who since spring had put the French commander Marshal Ferdinand Foch in control of their combined forces as Allied Supreme Commander, planned to push the Germans back in a series of battles collectively known as the Hundred Days Offensive. Now answering to Foch rather than to politicians at home, Douglas Haig came up with the plan to attack at the Somme, which the commander accepted over other locations. The Battle of Amiens commenced on 8th August. There was now close co-ordination between artillery, infantry, tanks and aircraft. Crucially, there was

also such tight secrecy that the Germans were completely surprised by the attack. They were pushed back creating a 15 mile gap in their lines and allowing the plans of their formidable Hindenburg Line to fall into Allied hands. This proved useful as British, Canadian, Australian, French and American forces closed into range of it by early September. The Germans lost most of the land they had captured that spring in a matter of four weeks. At the end of the month the Allies launched a series of attacks on the Hindenburg Line, breaking through to create around a 20 mile gap in the middle by 5th October.

By this time the Germans were also facing severe problems at home. This was in part created by restricted imports due to the Allied blockade of German ports. Rationing and various economic schemes had failed to quell discontent and rioting occurred across the Central Powers as their people suffered. It was estimated that by the end of 1918, over 400,000 Germans had died of starvation. With some decisive victories for the Allies and failing morale within German ranks their High Command saw no alternative other than to seek terms for an armistice. At around 5 am on 11th November 1918, in a train shunted onto a railway siding in the Forest of Compiègne, the Armistice was signed to take effect at 11 am on that eleventh day of the eleventh month. Although news spread quickly, fighting seems to have intensified that day and tragically thousands still died in the hours leading up to the designated time. Private George Edwin Ellison was the last British soldier to be killed and the Canadian Private George Lawrence Price was the final death from the Commonwealth forces at 10.58 am. An American soldier, Henry Gunther, was the last soldier to die. He charged a German machine gun post, despite them waving him back and initially refusing to fire. He was shot dead when he had got within a few yards of their position at 10.59 am.

Due to the destructive nature of the conflict, there is no exact figure for the numbers killed in the First World War. However, it is estimated that around 900,000 British soldiers died and over 1,600,000 were wounded. There were around 200,000 fatalities from the Commonwealth countries of Australia, New Zealand, Canada India and South Africa and 450,000 injured. The French Empire lost nearly one and a half million men and suffered over four million wounded, besides having the north-eastern corner of their country decimated with around 300,000 civilians dying from military action, disease and famine. Germany lost nearly two million soldiers with double that figure injured. The total deaths of all nations who fought in the war is around 8.5 million and 21 million wounded.

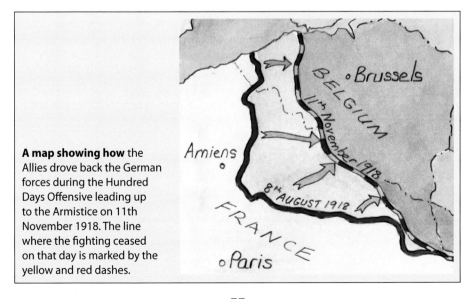

A map showing how the Allies drove back the German forces during the Hundred Days Offensive leading up to the Armistice on 11th November 1918. The line where the fighting ceased on that day is marked by the yellow and red dashes.

Returning Home

Over five million men from Britain and her colonies had served at some point on the Western Front during the First World War, with another two million in the Middle East and another million in various other countries around the globe. Those who were left at the end of hostilities could not just pack up their bags and leave, it would take time to process and demobilise the huge numbers of men. Regular soldiers who were still employed by the army received a new posting. Volunteers or conscripts with skills which were in short supply were initially the first to be sent home. But as soon as Winston Churchill became the new War Secretary in January 1919, he changed the policy so those who had signed up first were given priority. This helped to defuse the anger felt by long suffering soldiers waiting to return home. Frustration had already boiled over with mutiny, strikes and even riots, some with fatal consequences, breaking out.

Returning soldiers were first medically examined and then sent to a transit camp before sailing to Britain. They would then stay in a dispersal camp before being finally released to catch a train back home. For the hundreds of thousands who had served from Canada, Australia, South Africa, New Zealand and the other colonies they faced a much longer journey. It was a huge logistical task to organise the thousands of ships required to sail them home, while ports struggled to cope with the transit of such vast numbers of troops. Despite the mammoth task which faced the authorities nearly all of those who had volunteered or been conscripted were home by the end of 1919.

Life for those returning from the conflict could be tortuous and traumatic. Many suffered shell shock or had to live with wounds and disabilities. For some the horror of what they had gone through and their loss of dignity and self esteem was just too much and they became broken men. Families were ripped apart by the loss of a husband during the war or by the suffering of casualties after it was over. These losses were felt by all classes; with the acceleration in the selling off of country estates in the 1920s and 30s often being related to the loss of the young male heir during the First World War.

Partly due to a fear of revolution, as had occurred in Russia in 1917 and Germany shortly before the end of the war, the Government tried to bring in measures to improve life for the returning men. Many of those who had served still lived in slum conditions. Schemes like, 'Homes

Fit for Heroes' were introduced which encouraged local authorities to erect council housing. After the initial jubilation of the victory it began to sink in to many that the traditional markets for British goods had either shifted their sources of supply elsewhere or were financially broken. Many traditional industries suffered and unemployment became a major issue, especially after the global crisis in the wake of the Great Depression of 1929. Those returning men who had found work in the newer light industries such as electrical appliances, aircraft and motor car manufacturing, could benefit from lower costs and even buy their own house for the first time. Others however, returning to work in the old heavy industries, found their jobs had gone or would not last. As these industries were often based in the north and west of the country it was those areas which suffered most during the interwar years.

Remembering the Dead

In Britain, War Memorials were erected in every city and town as well as most villages. They not only recorded the great loss of life but acted as a timely reminder to future generations; there were only around 50 villages in the whole country to which all of the men returned alive. Many memorials were based upon the form of the Edwin Lutyens'

Cenotaph in Whitehall. Its simple and dignified form influenced similar memorials around the Empire. Most in Britain recorded those from the community who had failed to return, with the funding raised by subscription, others were private memorials paid for by a grieving family. Another type of memorial involved decommissioned tanks, given to towns and cities by the National War Savings Committee, in recognition of their contribution to the fundraising efforts during the conflict. These were usually placed in municipal parks or town centres, sometimes on a concrete or stone plinth. However, they do not seem to have been very popular as most were removed in the 1930s or broken up for their metal during the Second World War (one still survives in Ashford, Kent).

No special plans had been drawn up to record the names or graves of those killed as the war had developed. It was a Red Cross commander, Sir Fabian Ware, who was so appalled by the vast numbers that had been killed that he arranged for his unit to begin recording and looking after graves, later helping to establish the Imperial War Graves Commission. By the time the Armistice was signed, the Red Cross had already confirmed that around one million military personnel from around the British Empire had died in the

The Cenotaph, Whitehall, London:
Sir Edwin Lutyens had only a few weeks to design and erect a memorial in Whitehall for the Victory Parade, planned for the 19th July 1919. It was built of wood and plaster with the form of a coffin at the very top and wreathes at either end. The Allied commanders, Douglas Haig, John Pershing and Ferdinand Foch, turned and saluted it as they passed by on the day. Lutyens' dignified and simple design caught the public imagination. It was rebuilt in stone the following year in time for Remembrance Day and the two minute silence, which was the suggestion of King George V. This permanent Cenotaph (from the Greek word *kenotaphion* meaning empty tomb) now serves as a memorial to all the military dead from the British Empire in the First World War, Second World War and later conflicts.

conflict, with around 60 % along the Western Front alone. Some 587,000 graves were identified but a further 559,000 casualties were either laid to rest without identification or their bodies lost under the debris and mud of the battlefield. The Commission then established land for cemeteries along the Western Front and arranged for leading architects to plan these sites and design memorials, with Rudyard Kipling advising upon the inscriptions. Over 2400 of these were laid out across France and Belgium through the 1920s. In addition, a number of memorials to the missing were erected. The first to be completed was the Menin Gate Memorial at Ypres (today known as Ieper), designed by Sir Reginald Blomfield, with the names of over 55,000 soldiers recorded as missing inscribed upon it. Tyne Cot in Belgium by Sir Herbert Baker and the Thiepval Memorial on the Somme by Sir Edwin Lutyens soon followed.

Memorials were also raised by the other countries who served under the banner of the British Empire, to their soldiers who were killed or lost during the conflict. While many chose to raise memorials in their own country, others placed their principal memorial on the Western Front, at the site where they had suffered their first or greatest loss.

The Australians raised theirs at Villers-Bretonneux, the South Africans at Delville Wood, the Canadians at Vimy Ridge and the Newfoundlanders at Beaumont-Hamel. As these countries forged their own identities and independence, not least as a result of the sacrifice of their men during the conflict, their memorials are greatly revered. There are of course many German war cemeteries along the Western Front. They differ in design to the British or French ones, being simpler and more austere; often built around lawns but with little decoration. They symbolise well the tragedy of the conflict.

Rebuilding and Removing the Signs of War

All along the Western Front civilians returned home to discover what remained of their homes. Many towns, villages and farms had been flattened and their rich agricultural land destroyed by trenches, craters and tunnelling. The French government actively sought reparation payments from Germany, in part to pay for the massive reconstruction task. The medieval city of Ypres, which by the end of the war lay in ruins, had been largely rebuilt by the 1930s. The greatest problem came from the unexploded shells, grenades and mines which posed a lethal threat to those trying to rebuild or work the land. Farmers were often killed when this ordnance exploded, especially when tractors were introduced in the 1930s. One of the huge mines buried at Hill 60 (page 69) exploded suddenly in 1955 when it was hit during a thunder storm. Incredibly, even today the French Department of Mine Clearance still collects and destroys over 900 tonnes of ammunition each year and over 600 clearers have been killed since 1945.

The trenches, which had been home for millions of soldiers of all sides during the war, were either ploughed up by farmers or filled in to make way for new roads and buildings. However, on some sectors of the front which were regarded as too dangerous, had little agricultural value, or were retained as part of memorials, the earthwork defences can still be seen today. Signs of these features can also be made out on aerial photographs or as lines of different coloured soil in ploughed fields. Concrete bunkers often survive and can still be seen today around the countryside. Sadly, the remains of those who were killed are also still occasionally found during building work; 250 British and Australian soldiers who died during the Battle of Fromelles were discovered in 2009, necessitating the building of a new cemetery.

The First World War Today

Attitudes towards the war have changed over the decades. Initially, while seen in Britain as a great victory it was at the same time viewed as a horrific conflict which many preferred to forget. There could be no huge outpouring of victorious celebration as there were so many in mourning for lost loved ones. After the Second World War, views hardened and concentrated on the futility of the earlier war, with particular criticism levelled at how the soldiers had been poorly

---

The Treaty of Versailles

In January 1919 the representatives from over thirty nations met in Paris to hammer out a peace treaty. Initially, when the Germans had signed the Armistice they had agreed that any resolution should follow the 'Fourteen Points' proposed by American President Woodrow Wilson earlier in the year. However, the British Prime Minister David Lloyd George had just won a General Election under the banner, 'Make Germany Pay' (Britain had very much drained its reserves to pay for the war). The French Prime, Minister Georges Clemenceau, whose people wanted the enemy weakened so they could not threaten France again, also had other ideas. After months of heated wrangling, a treaty was finally drawn up and presented to the Germans. It required the payment of billions of pounds for the damage caused, cut their army back in size, denied them an airforce and gave away their former colonies and parts of the country to the victorious nations. Yet it was not these reparations and limitations which alone riled the Germans, it was Article 231 which stated that the war was imposed upon the Allies as a consequence of the aggression of Germany and her allies that aroused real anger. The War Guilt Clause as it became known, fuelled hostility to the treaty. In the end only part of the reparation payment was ever received; the loans which Germany took out to finance these payments were only paid off in 2010. Germany also felt, as it had won in Russia and almost won on the Western Front, that it had not been honourably defeated. A feeling grew that their brave soldiers had been let down by factions opposed to the war at home, with the Jewish population ominously taking the brunt of these malicious rumours.

In the USA, Wilson tried to support the peace treaty but suffered a stroke that effectively ended his leadership. The opponents to his cause won the next election and made their own treaty with Germany. The conditions set out at Versailles were also renegotiated a number of times before parts were put on hold indefinitely or simply ignored. The inability of the Allies to work closely together in the aftermath of the war is seen today as the main cause of later troubles, along with the effects of the Great Depression which gripped the world in the early 1930s and helped the Nazis under Adolf Hitler to gain control of Germany in 1933. As the Allied Supreme Commander, the French Marshal Foch stated after the treaty had been signed, 'This is not a peace but an armistice for twenty years.' He was right as the Second World War started precisely twenty years after it had been signed.

led in comparison with the later conflict. However, in recent decades historians have reviewed official documents which were not available to previous generations. A more informed analysis of the decisions made by commanders has been produced. No one doubts the horrors of the war and the tragic loss of life, but those who sent them to their deaths were seen to be doing the best they could within the limited tools at their command, and against a form and scale of war that they had never faced before.

Despite a century having now passed since the blood bath on the Western Front the events between 1914 and 1918 still have relevance today. Military and political overconfidence that a war would be quick with little need for preparation should things go wrong has been repeated a number of times since. The First World War resulted in the dismantling of many European Empires. It also encouraged the demands from their dominions for self-government. Another crucial consequence was that the war, like all wars, was hugely expensive. It created national debts that crippled economies and gave rise to a generation trapped in financial depression. Perhaps most importantly, what at the time was referred to as the Great War, was not, 'The war to end all wars'.

The Nicholson War Memorial, Leek, Staffs: An example of a major war memorial raised in this small mill town to the memory of the men of Leek who lost their lives in the First World War. It was paid for by Sir Arthur and Lady Nicholson who lost their son in July 1915. The names of the soldiers who did not return are listed on two bronze plaques and the battles in which they fought are carved around the top just above the clock. You can find more information and a video showing its unveiling ceremony in 1925 at www.nicholsonmemorial.org.uk.

The Origins of the First World War

The Assassination of Archduke Franz Ferdinand

On 28th June 1914, the Bosnian Serb nationalist society the Black Hand saw the perfect opportunity to revolt against the rule of the Austro-Hungarian Empire by assassinating the heir to its throne, Franz Ferdinand.

While Archduke Franz Ferdinand and his wife were on a formal visit to the Bosnian capital of Sarajevo, six members of the Black Hand group lined the route. Their plan was to kill the royal couple as their open top car drove past. One of the group, Nedeljko Čabrinović, threw a grenade towards the car. However, he forgot about the timed delay it exploded under a vehicle further back in the cavalcade injuring the driver. Nedeljko, trying to take his own life, first swallowed poison then threw himself into the river Miljacka. Unfortunately for him, the poison only made him sick while the river was just 10cm deep. He was promptly arrested by the authorities. The remaining conspirators fled in the resulting commotion, assuming their opportunity had passed.

One of the group, Gavrilo Princip, made his way to a local tavern. As luck would have it though, the Archduke insisted that he should visit the hospital to see the injured driver. To avoid the risk of a further assassination attempt he chose to take a different route and avoid the city centre. His chauffeur got lost, drove down a one way street and, while trying to reverse, stalled the engine.

Gavrilo Princip: This slight of a man, born in 1894 to an impoverished Bosnian family, was described by a major in the Serbian Army when he tried to join up as 'too small and too weak'. This however seems to have inspired Gavrilo to prove his doubters wrong by performing a daring act, one which would trigger a sequence of events resulting in the First World War.

In an incredible piece of coincidence, the car stopped outside the very tavern where a disheartened Gavrilo was sitting drinking. The young Bosnian made the most of this unexpected opportunity, pulled a pistol from his pocket, strode up to the open top car and shot dead Franz Ferdinand and his wife, Sophie.

The Emergence of a Unified Germany

To understand why such a comparatively minor incident away from the main flow of European politics should result in such a catastrophic war, we need to look back over the previous fifty years to see how tensions and jealousies had grown between the major countries.

In the 1860s, Europe had been dominated by France, Spain and Great Britain in the west and Russia, Austria-Hungary and the Ottoman Empire in the east, with smaller countries and independent territories sandwiched between them.

However, the balance of power began to change when the German state of Prussia defeated first Austria in July 1866, and then France in 1871. In the latter conflict the separate German states fell in line behind the Prussian forces to form a new united German Empire under Otto von Bismarck, who was first Chancellor of Prussia and then Chancellor of the German Empire, and Kaiser Wilhelm I (Kaiser is the German title for Emperor).

A close up of the Balkan region with countries which would become part of the Central Powers along with Germany coloured orange and those which would support the Allies in yellow. The Balkans had been part of the Ottoman Empire but as it weakened from the mid-19th century so countries sought their independence.

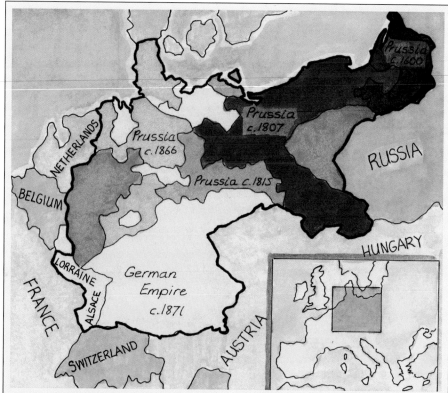

A map showing how Prussia progressively expanded from its 16th century homeland (marked in darkest red) outwards to finally include the southern German states and the French acquisitions in 1871 (marked in yellow) and become the German Empire .

The conflict with the French had been brief and its success was partly due to the new German command structure, with its detailed planning, powerful artillery and universal conscription. The French were forced to cede their border territory of Alsace and part of Lorraine to the new German Empire, and this became a source of lingering resentment.

The new unified Germany was quick to establish itself as a prominent industrial power under Bismarck and Wilhelm I. Upon the death of Wilhelm in March 1888,

his more liberal minded son Frederick III (who was married to Queen Victoria's eldest daughter) became Emperor. However, he died of cancer after a reign of only 99 days. Instead, his son Wilhelm II became Emperor, determined to create a powerful new navy to rival that of Britain. The Kaiser also drew Germany into a number of foreign issues and conflicts, without actually going to war. His country's colonial ambitions, especially in Africa, its growing industrial might and interference in global politics created tensions within Europe.

After the humiliation of the 1870-1871 war with Prussia, the French analysed where they had gone wrong. They rebuilt a powerful army and put plans in place so that should the opportunity arise they could strike quickly to gain back the territory they had lost.

The Austro-Hungarian Empire was centuries old but it was on the wane, especially after the defeat by the Prussians in 1866. It was also facing problems; in some of its territory there were complex ethnic disputes that were tearing it apart from within.

Despite strong royal links with Germany and Russia, Great Britain stood back from these mid-19th century European conflicts and focused upon building industry, financial wealth and trade with its huge Empire. It maintained the most powerful navy in the world to protect its merchant fleet and territories, but had only needed a small army to deal with colonial disputes.

As with its neighbours in the west, Russia sought to expand its boundaries and under Tsar Nicholas II made attempts to push into Korea. However, it came up against a dynamic new nation, Japan. They drove the Russians back on land and at the Battle of the Tsushima Strait destroyed the Russian Fleet; of the thirty-eight warships which entered it only three made it back to a port.

This placed Japan on the world stage and highlighted to the Germans the value of a strong navy.

A Tangled Web of Alliances

With growing tensions between the European powers, countries began to form treaties in order to protect themselves from colonial expansion, commercial threat or the military might of their neighbours.

Kaiser Wilhelm II: This erratic and militaristic monarch was the key figure in creating the tensions which resulted in the First World War. He was intelligent and appreciated modern technology and industry but had a short attention span and an explosive temper, rarely looking deeply into a problem and often making ill-judged comments. Shortly after becoming Emperor he dismissed Bismarck, the man who had nurtured a fragile peace between the new Germany and its neighbours and with his steadying hand now gone other countries began looking to sign treaties as fear and suspicion grew over the intentions of the Kaiser. Despite acting in such a clumsy and aggressive way towards neighbouring powers he does seem to have been hesitant about going to war against them and became rather sidelined as the conflict developed.

Bismarck understood that Germany's priority was to form alliances to maintain stability. He was also keen to ensure that France remained isolated to avoid Germany from facing enemies on two fronts, France in the west and Russia in the east. He knew that France wanted revenge for their earlier loss of Alsace and Lorraine. In 1873, Bismarck negotiated the Three Emperors League, which united Germany, Austria-Hungary and Russia in time of war. In 1878, Russia withdrew and the new Dual Alliance between Germany and Austria-Hungary was agreed in 1879. The two powers agreed to stand together if either nation were attacked.

Italy, which had unified around the same time as Germany, joined Germany and Austria-Hungary in 1881 to create a Triple Alliance. Twenty years later though, Italy came to a secret agreement with France to remain neutral should Germany attack France. In 1915, Italy entered the First World War as an ally of Britain, France and Russia.

Bismarck agreed a Reinsurance Treaty with Russia in 1887 where both powers agreed to remain neutral if either were at war.

However, in 1890 Bismarck was dismissed by the German Kaiser Wilhlem II and this useful alliance was abandoned. Instead, the Russians made an alliance with France in 1894 which stipulated that if a member of the Triple Alliance of Germany, Austria-Hungary and Italy attacked either of them (Russia or France) then they would use force against the aggressor in question.

Britain increasingly found itself isolated and concerned about German threats to its markets, so the new King, Edward VII, was sent on a charm offensive to France. In 1904, the two nations signed an Entente Cordiale, agreeing to closer diplomatic co-operation. In 1907, a similar understanding with Russia was signed and the three nations formed a Triple Entente, which would form the basis of the Allied forces when war broke out.

Thus most of the main European powers were tied together into two main camps and all it would take was for one to threaten another for the fuse attached to the treaties to become lit and war to break out. The spark which ignited this chain reaction was provided by Gavrilo Princip, on 28th June 1914.

Places to Visit

Museums in France and Belgium

There are numerous museums, memorials and cemeteries in France and Belgium worthy of a visit by anyone interested in the First World War. The following websites hold information on locating them and the list below is of some of the more notable sites which contain information or reconstructions of the trenches:

www.greatwar.co.uk
www.ww1battlefields.co.uk
www.ypres-1917.com
www.somme-battlefields.com
www.ww1cemeteries.com
www.cwgc.org

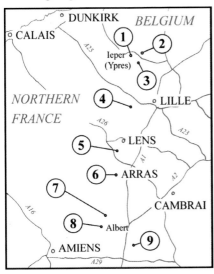

1: In Flanders Fields Museum and the Menin Gate, Ieper

Ieper, formerly better known by its French name Ypres, was the scene of three major battles during the war and was virtually flattened by the end of the conflict. Its rebuilding afterwards was financed by German reparations and it became a sacred centre for the British in memory of the suffering and loss of life during the conflict. Today you can visit the impressive Menin Gate Memorial to the Missing (Meensestraat) and the In Flanders Fields Museum just up the road in the rebuilt Medieval Cloth Hall (Grote Markt 34). www.inflandersfields.be

2: Memorial Museum Passchendaele 1917 and Tyne Cot Cemetery, Zonnebeke

Just outside Ieper in the village of Zonnebeke is a museum dedicated to the Third Battle of Ypres, better known as the Battle of Passchendaele. This offensive in 1917 resulted in a huge loss of life amongst British and Colonial troops and the Tyne Cot Cemetery (Vijfwegenstraat 1, 8980 Zonnebeke) is the largest for Commonwealth Troops in the world. The museum in the village (B.Pilstraat 5a, B-8980 Zonnebeke) is one of the finest dedicated to the First World War with reconstructed trenches and dugouts, in addition to an impressive collection of artefacts. www.passchendaele.be

3: Hill 62 - Sanctuary Wood Trench Museum, Zillebeke, Ieper

This section of battlefield was preserved immediately after the war by the grandfather of the present owner. Although the defences have seen a lot of work since to repair them, they are a unique glimpse of actual trenches and tunnels with an accompanying museum containing 3D photographs (Canadalaan 26, 8900 Zillebeke).

4: Fromelles (Pheasant Wood) Military Cemetery and Museum, France

The relatively small area of the battlefield and the village here makes Fromelles a good, representative place from where an understanding of the Western Front as a whole can be gained. It was a diversionary battle as part of the Somme Offensive but it was rushed and largely failed with the loss of over 5000 mostly Australian troops. At Pheasant Wood a new cemetery was opened in 2010 after a mass grave containing hundreds of Australian and British soldiers was discovered. There is also a new visitor centre part-funded by the Australian Government, the V.C. Corner Australian Cemetery and Memorial (Rue Delval) and an excellent museum in the village hall (10 rue d'Eglise, 59 Fromelles). At the time of writing a new and larger museum is under construction.

5: Canadian National Vimy Memorial

The Battle of Vimy Ridge in April 1917, part of the Battle of Arras, was the first time all four divisions of the Canadian forces fought as one and is seen as a defining moment in the history of the nation. After the war, the Canadian government secured a 250 acre tract of land at Vimy Ridge and erected a graceful memorial dedicated to those Canadians who had lost their lives during the conflict. The site has been magnificently maintained and manned by Canadian forces ever since and the trenches and battlefield, which have been left untouched, can still be seen today. A Must Visit site. (Chemin des Canadiens (Route D55) 62580 Vimy, Pas-de-Calais). www.veterans.gc.ca/eng/memorials/france/vimy

6: The Wellington Quarry, Memorial of the Battle of Arras

In the build up to the Battle of Arras in 1917 a vast complex of tunnels was dug under the town linking up old underground workings to house thousands of troops in order to surprise the enemy. An underground museum (rue Arthur Delétoile, 62000 Arras) has now been opened in one of the sections, named by the New Zealand troops who were responsible for much of the tunnelling after their capital, Wellington. Visitors can go on guided tours of this incredible site and also see a short film about the battle. www.explorearras.com/en/visit/remembrance

7: Thiepval Memorial to the Missing of the Somme

This largest of the British war memorials, designed by Sir Edwin Lutyens, was erected to the memory of over 70,000 missing troops who died on the Somme Battlefield during the war. The new visitor centre at the site (rue de l'Ancre, 80300 Thiepval) uses short films and displays to put the memorial and the battle into context. To the south east at Longueval is the Delville Wood South African National Memorial and cemetery. www.thiepval.org.uk

8: Musée Somme 1916, Albert

An atmospheric museum built in underground tunnels which uses artefacts found in the surrounding area and an authentic reconstruction of trenches to show what life was like for soldiers during the Battle of the Somme (rue Anicet Godin, 80300 Albert). www.musee-somme-1916.eu

9: Historial de la Grande Guerre (Museum of the Great War), Péronne

This impressive museum contains artefacts, memorabilia, posters and films from the conflict to tell the story of life for troops and civilians on all sides. Château de Péronne, BP 20063, 80201 Péronne. www.historial.org

Museums in Britain

There are also a number of museums in the UK which have memorabilia and reconstructions of trenches. The Imperial War Museum and its website www.iwm.org.uk is an excellent starting point. Many regiments and corps have their own museums some of which have special displays, events and reconstructions of trenches. www.armymuseums.org.uk

Imperial War Museum

Lambeth Road, London SE1 6HZ
www.iwm.org.uk
Tel: 0207 416 5000

National Army Museum

Royal Hospital Road, Chelsea,
London SW3 4HT
www.nam.ac.uk
Tel: 0207 730 0717

Royal Engineers Museum

Prince Arthur Road,
Gillingham, Kent ME4 4UG
www.re-museum.co.uk
Tel: 01634 822839

Somme Heritage Centre

233 Bangor Road, Newtownards,
County Down BT23 7PH Northern Ireland
www.irishsoldier.org
Tel: 0289 182 3202

The Tank Museum

Bovington, Dorset, BH20 6JG
www.tankmuseum.org
Tel: 01929 405096

Fort Widley

Portsdown Hill Road,
Portsmouth, Hants PO6 3LS
www.visitportsmouth.co.uk/things-to-do/
world-war-1-remembrance-centre-p963841
Tel: 0239 279 8751

Staffordshire Regiment Museum

Whittington Barracks,
Lichfield WS14 9PY
staffordshireregimentmuseum.com
Tel: 01543 434394/434395

Other Useful Websites

Wikipedia is a very informative starting point when researching any detail of the war. The following sites may also prove useful:

www.worldwar1.com
www.1914-1918.net
www.firstworldwar.com/
www.pals.org.uk/
www.fylde.demon.co.uk/welcome.htm

Glossary of Terms

Accessory: British cylinder-discharged gas was called this in order to keep its use secret.

Artillery: large calibre guns used on land.

Bantam: Soldiers under 5'5" in height who would previously have been deemed as too short to enlist.

Barbed wire: Twisted wire with short sharp barbs entwined within it. Military barbed wire had the barbs set closer together than agricultural types.

Bomber: A specialist trained in the use of hand grenades, known as grenadier earlier in the war but after May 1916 as a bomber after the Grenadier Guards protested.

Brodie: British steel helmet introduced in 1916 and invented by John L Brodie.

Bully beef: Tinned corned beef, one of the staple rations of the British Army.

Bunker: An underground shelter.

Calibre: The diameter of the barrel of a gun or rifle.

Chit: A slip or receipt from the Hindustani 'cittha' meaning a note.

Civvy: A civilian.

Corkscrew: A steel post with a corkscrew end which could be quietly twisted into the ground when staking out barbed wire so the enemy could not hear.

Daisy cutter: A shell with an impact fuse which exploded on contact with anything above ground and was used to clear barbed wire entrapments.

Duckboards: Slatted wooden boards raised above the bottom of the trench to keep it dry.

Dug-out: An underground shelter.

Entrenching tool: Typically a spade and pick in one, carried as part of the soldier's kit.

Fire step: A step on the enemy side of the trench onto which rifle men stepped up to fire through gaps in the parapet.

Fritz: Another name for a German which came from the popular name Friedrich.

Funk: Someone who was in a state of fear, nervousness, or depression.

Funk-hole: Small dug-out or shelter in the wall of a trench.

Glory hole: A dug-out.

Go west: To be killed.

Grass-cutter: Small bombs dropped from planes which scattered shrapnel balls at low-level upon impact with the intention of killing or maiming soldiers.

Hun: After the Kaiser urged his troops to behave like Attilla's Huns in order to strike fear into the enemy this became a nickname for the Germans.

Jakes: An old name for toilets or latrines.

Jam-tins: Improvised hand grenades and bombs made in jam tins early in the war.

Jerry: Another term for a German which was popular later in the war.

Land ship or creeper: A tank.

Loophole: Gap or hole in the parapet through which a rifle could be fired.

Machine gun: A gun which fired rounds in rapid succession, by this time using the power of the previous shot to move the next round into place.

Mad minute: Firing off fifteen or more rounds of rapid aimed shots from a bolt action Lee Enfield rifle in one minute.

Magazine: A container with rounds which is inserted into a rifle or machine gun.

Mills bomb: An egg-shaped hand grenade with square grooves, invented by William Mills in 1915. It remained in use until the 1960s.

Mob: Battalion or other unit.

Mustard gas: Distinctive yellow coloured gas which incapacitated soldiers with blistering and burns.

Over the top: Going over the parapet on ladders when making an attack.

Panzer: A German tank, shortened from their full title Sturmpanzerkampfwagen.

Parapet: The raised wall on the front of a trench typically made from sandbags.

Phosgene: A type of poison gas.

Picket: A metal post used for holding barbed wire.

Pillbox: A German concrete gun emplacement named because it looked like a pill box, a small tin for tablets, which was sometimes used by the Allies.

Pushing up daisies: Dead and buried.

Revetment: Timber boards, metal sheeting, brushwood, sandbags or similar materials used to hold back the exposed mud sides of a trench.

Round: The bullet and the propellant which fired it out of a gun or rifle. A single shot in effect was a single round.

Sandbags: Sacks or bags filled with sand, clay or mud to make pillow-shaped lumps which were used like bricks to make the parapet or sides of a trench.

Sap: A hole at the end of a narrow trench built out into No Man's Land from the front line so men could listen to the enemy or use it as a launching point for a raid or attack.

Sapper: A private soldier in the Royal Engineers. They were originally the diggers of saps.

Shell: A hollow metal pointed case which contained an explosive and was fired from guns and howitzers.

Shrapnel: Metal balls ejected from a shell of the same name; used to take out men and horses on the battlefield and named after its inventor General H Shrapnel. Often used to describe any metal fragments from other types of shell.

Slack: Small pieces of debris thrown up by a shell bursting on the ground.

Star shell: A projectile with a magnesium flare which lit up the battlefield when it exploded.

Ticket: An official discharge from the army often for medical reasons.

Toffee apple: A type of mortar bomb with attached wooden shaft.

Tracer: A rifle or machine gun round which left a red trail so its flight could be observed.

Whippet: A lighter form of British tank named after the fast running breed of dog and later applied to all light tanks.

Whizz bang: A high-velocity shell named after the noise it made in flight and when exploding.

Yperite: French name for mustard gas.

Index

A

Accrington Pals	31-32
Amiens, Battle of	76
Armistice	76-77, 82
Arras, Battle of	54, 69, 90
Artillery	49, 51, 52, 55-67
Asquith, Herbert Henry	50

B

Baker, Sir Herbert	80
Bayonets	41, 63
Beaumont-Hamel Newfoundland Memorial	81
Bismarck, Otto von	85-88
Black Hand	84
Bloch, Jan Gotlib	17
Blomfield , Sir Reginald	80
Brodie, John L.	65

C

Čabrinović, Nedeljko	84
Cambrai, Battle of	72
Canadian National Vimy Memorial	81, 90
Cannons	53, 55
Cavalry	48, 51
Cenotaph	79-80
Chamberlain, Neville	74
Churchill, Winston	47, 50, 78
Clemenceau, Georges Benjamin	82
Coltman, Lance Corporal William V.C.	27

D

Delville Wood South African National Memorial	81

E

Edward VII, King	88
Ellison, Private George Edwin	77
Entente Cordiale	12, 88

F

Ferdinand, Archduke Franz	12, 84
Fiedler, Richard	69
Flamethrowers	32, 48, 69

Foch, Marshal Ferdinand	76, 80, 82
Frederick III, Kaiser	86
French, Sir John	29, 51
Fromelles, Battle of	81
Fromelles (Pheasant Wood) Military Cemetery	90

G

Gallipolli Campaign	50, 64
Gas	29, 32-33, 39-41, 43, 46, 67-68
George V, King	80
George, David Lloyd	50, 58, 82
Gotha G.V.	56
Grenades	53, 62
Grenfell, Captain Julian	15
Gunther, Sergeant Henry N.	77

H

Haig, Field Marshal Sir Douglas	29, 42, 49, 51, 55, 76, 80
Hill 60	69, 81
Hill 62 (Sanctuary Wood) Memorial	90
Hindenburg Line	18, 45, 76
Hitler, Adolf	73-74, 82
Howitzer	58-59
Hundred Days Offensive	76-77

I

Imperial War Graves Commission	79-80

K

Kipling, Rudyard	80
Kitchener, Lord Horatio	12, 29, 31

L

Lawrence, Thomas Edward	50
Lewis, Isaac Newton	67
Lewis light machine gun	67
Lusitania	45
Lutyens, Sir Edwin Landseer	79-80, 91

M

Machine guns	65-67
Machine Gun Corps	66

McCrae, Lieutenant Colonel
  John Alexander 30
Menin Gate Memorial to the Missing 80, 89
Military Service Act, 1916 36
Mills grenade 62
Mining 69
Miracle of the Marne 14
Moltke, Helmuth von 13
Mortars 60-63

N
National War Savings Committee 79
Nicholas II, Tsar 87
Nicholson War Memorial 83
Nivelle, Commander in Chief
  Robert Georges 54

O
Owen, Wilfred 52

P
Passchendaele 54-55, 89
Pershing, Brigadier General John J. 80
Pétain, Commander in Chief Philippe 54
Plan 17 13
Price, Private George Lawrence 77
Princess Mary's Gift Box 15
Princip, Gavrilo 84, 88

R
Race to the Sea 14
Red Cross 79
Richthofen, Manfred von 56
Rickman, Lieutenant Colonel
  Arthur Wilmot 31
Rifles 63-65
Royal Air Force 56
Royal Army Medical Corps 44
Royal Flying Corps 56

S
Sassoon, Siegfried 52
Schlieffen, Count Alfred von 13
Schlieffen Plan 13
Shell Shock 37, 40
Signal Corps 53
Skeyhill, Private Tom 46
Somme, Battle of 31-32, 42, 46, 65, 70

Spring Offensive, 1918 74-75
Staffordshire Regiment Museum 27
Stokes Mortar 61
Stokes, Sir Wilfred 61
Submarines 45
Swinton, Colonel 47

T
Tandey, Private Henry 73-74
Tanks 47-48, 51, 53, 70-72, 76, 79
Tank Corps 71
Thiepval Memorial to the Missing
  of the Somme 80, 91
Treaty of Versailles 82
Trench Foot 19, 40-41
Tritton, Sir William 47, 70
Tyne Cot Commonwealth War
  Graves Cemetery and Memorial
  to the Missing 80, 89

V
Villers-Bretonneux Memorial 81

W
War Horse 5, 48
Ware, Sir Fabian 79
Wheeler, Private Victor 28
Wilhelm I, Kaiser 85-86
Wilhelm II, Kaiser 12, 86-88
Wilson, Major Walter Gordon 47, 70
Wilson, Thomas Woodrow 82

Y
Ypres 32, 89
Ypres, The First Battle of 29, 51
Ypres, The Second Battle of 29
Ypres, The Third Battle of
  (Passchendaele) 54, 69

Z
Zeppelins 56

The Poppy

THE RED FIELD POPPY has seeds which can remain dormant for many years, so when the fields of northern France were churned up by fighting it was this resilient flower which burst into bloom around the trenches in spring and early summer. Inspired by John McCrae's poem (see page 30) an American Moina Michael, who was working for the YMCA in November 1918, thought the flower would make a suitable emblem of remembrance. She promoted it in America. At the same time a representative of the French YMCA, Anna Guérin, who had seen Moina's poppy, used the idea to raise money by selling cloth versions in the war torn areas of her country. It was Anna who had a meeting with Sir Douglas Haig, the founder of The British Legion, and convinced him that the poppy should be adopted as its emblem. Since 1921 they have been sold from mid October to raise funds in support of its charitable work.

In 2014, The Tower of London decided to mark the 1914 onset of the Great War by creating a huge artwork of red, ceramic poppies within the great moat of the Tower. Each of the 888,246 flowers represented a British military fatality from the conflict.

The scale of the display reflected the magnitude of such an important centenary. It created a giant visual spectacle and at the same time offered a location for personal reflection. Its creator, the ceramic artist Paul Cummins felt that the poppies should then be removed after Armistice Day, reflecting the transient nature of the soldiers' lives that had ended at such an early age.

The success of the poppy field was proved by the huge crowds who gathered daily around the Tower, and on occasions caused local public and private transport to come to a halt. The poppies themselves were sold to members of the public with the proceeds going to a variety of service charities.